I0449498

PROBLEMS & SOLUTION

IN

PROTON NMR SPECTROSCOPY

Dr. Vinod Jena
(Government Nagarjuna P. G. College of Science, Raipur CG, INDIA)

Dr. M. L. Satnami
(SOS in Chemistry, Pt Ravishankar Shukla University Raipur CG, INDIA)

Dr. Natalija Matic
(Research Scientist Hrvatske Vode, Zagreb, CROATIA)

&

Dr. Marina Mlakar
(Senior Scientist, Ruđer Bošković Institute, Zagreb CROATIA

LP INC. PUBLISHER NORTH CAROLINA, USA
2016

LP INC. PUBLISHER NORTH CAROLINA, USA

First Printing: 2016

ISBN: 978-1-329-66983--3

DEDICATION

This book is dedicated to my best Professor, Dr. (Smt.) Rama Pande, Former Head of Department, School of Studies in Chemistry, Pt Ravishankar Shukla University Raipur, CG, India.
Without her blessings and inspiration, I would have never achieved to my dream.

(Vinod Jena)

Preface

NMR spectroscopy is arguably the most important analytical method available today. The reasons are manifold: it is applied by chemists and physicists to gases, liquids, liquid crystals and solids. Biochemists use it routinely for determining the structures of peptides and proteins, and it is also widely used in medicine (where it is often called MRI, Magnetic Resonance Imaging). It is however true to say that the structures of a wide variety of organic compounds can be solved using just NMR spectroscopy, which provides a huge arsenal of measurement techniques in one to three dimensions. To determine an organic structure using NMR data is however not always a simple task, depending on the complexity of the molecule. This book is intended to solve organic structures with the help of NMR spectra. It contains a series of problems, which to help the beginner.

This book containing collections of problems of different complexity are invaluable for students, since theory of itself is not very useful in deducing the structure from the spectra. This book is also very useful for UGC-CSIR NET, SET, SLET, & other competitive examinations

(Authors)

BASICS OF NMR

NMR- Nuclear Magnetic Resonance is a branch of spectroscopy that deals with the phenomenon found in assemblies of large number of nuclei of atoms that possess both "magnetic moments" and "angular momentum" is subjected to external magnetic field.

Resonance – Implies that we are in tune with a natural frequency of the nuclear magnetic system in the magnetic field.

Principles of ^{1}H NMR

Any motion of a charged particle has an associated magnetic field. This means, that a magnetic dipole is created, just like an electrical current in a loop creates a magnetic dipole, which in a magnetic field corresponds to a magnetic moment.

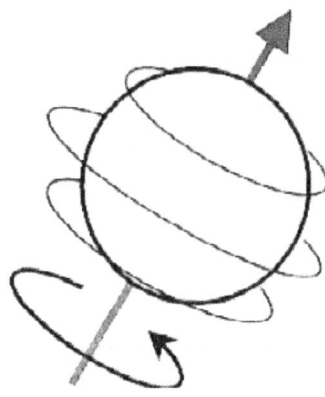

Figure1: A spinning nucleus can be regarded as a microscopic magnet.

1

The nucleus of hydrogen atom (proton) behaves as a spinning bar magnet because it possesses both electric and magnetic spin. The nucleus of H-atom generates a magnetic field. NMR involves the interaction between and oscillating magnetic field of electromagnetic radiation and the magnetic energy of the H-nucleus when these are placed in an external static magnetic field. The magnetic moment μ of a nucleus is intimately connected with its spin angular momentum (I). To be more precise μ is proportional to I, which is the angular momentum quantum number usually called the nuclear spin, with a proportionality constant γ known as gyromagnetic ratio:

$$\mu = \gamma I \quad \dots\dots\dots\dots\dots(i)$$

Larmor precession

According to classical motion of a magnetic moment, μ, in a uniform externally applied strong magnetic field B0 under the condition of constant total energy. The movement of μ traces out a cone about B_0, which is analogous to the motion of a gyroscope running in friction-free bearings under the influence of the Earth's field (Figure 2). Such motion   is referred to in general as Larmor precession. The precession frequency, v_0, is given by:

$$v_0 = |\gamma| B_0 / 2\pi \quad \dots\dots\dots\dots(ii)$$

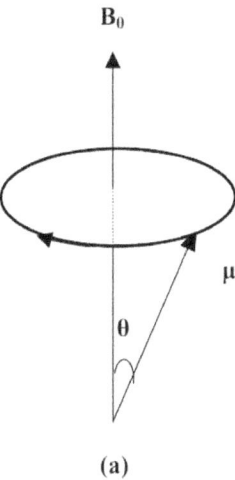

(a)

Figure 2: Precession of a magnetic moment μ about an applied magnetic field B₀.

Suppose there is an additional externally applied, but weak magnetic field, **B₁**, perpendicular to **B₀**. Such a field will also exert a torque on **μ**, tending to change the angle θ between **μ** and **B₀**. However, if **B₁** is fixed in direction and magnitude, it will alternately try to increase and decrease θ as **μ** precesses. Since **B₁** is stated to be weak, the net effect will be a slight wobbling in the precession of **μ**. Alternatively, the motion of **μ** can be described as caused by a resultant field **B₀** + **B₁**. If, on the other hand, **B1** is not fixed, but is rotating about **B₀** with the same frequency as the precession of **μ**, its orientation with respect to **μ** will be constant. Suppose this orientation is such, that **B₁** is always perpendicular to the plane containing **B₀** and **μ** as in **Figure 3**; then the torque exerted on **μ** by **B₁** will always be away from **B₀**

3

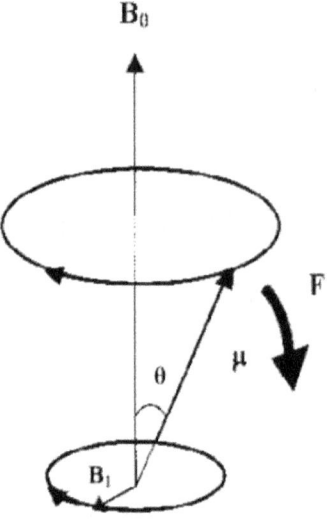

Figure 3: The effect of a rotating magnetic field, B_1, on a precessing magnetic moment, μ.

When B_1 is perpendicular to the B_1 - μ plane, there is a force F acting to increase the angle between B_0 and μ. If μ and B_1 are rotating at the same rate, this force acts always away from B_0 and therefore has a consistent effect. Consequently, an accumulated effect on μ is possible. Since changing θ corresponds to changing the energy of μ in B_0, this condition is described as resonance – the frequency, ν, of the field B_1 required must equal the Larmor precession frequency of equation (ii) . The energy for the change of θ is, of course, derived from the rotating field B_1, which is supplied by radio frequency electromagnetic radiation.

Quantum mechanical description

According to the classical picture the atomic nucleus, assumed to be spherical, rotates about an axis and thus, posses a nuclear or intrinsic angular momentum **P**. Quantum mechanical considerations show that, like many other atomic properties, this angular momentum is quantized:

$$\mathbf{P} = \hbar\sqrt{I(I + 1)}\ldots\ldots\ldots\ldots\text{(iii)}$$

where $\hbar = h/2\pi$, (h is Planck's constant). The nuclear spin can have values $\mathbf{I} = 0, 1/2, 1, 3/2, 2,\ldots\ldots\ldots$ up to 7. As it will be explained below, neither the values of $\mathbf{I}$ nor those of $\mathbf{P}$ can yet be predicted from theory. If a nucleus with angular momentum **P** and magnetic moment **μ** is placed in a static strong magnetic field **B0**, the angular momentum takes up an orientation such that its component **Pz** along the direction of the field is an integral or half-integral multiple of $\hbar$:

$$\mathbf{Pz} = \mathbf{m_I}\,\hbar \ldots\ldots\ldots\ldots\ldots\text{(iv)}$$

where mI is the magnetic or directional quantum number with values $m_I = I, I - 1,\ldots, -I$. It can easily be deduced that there are $(2I + 1)$ different values of mI, and consequently an equal number of possible orientations of the angular momentum and magnetic moment in an external magnetic field $\mathbf{B_0}$.

For ^{1}H and ^{13}C nuclei, which have $I = \frac{1}{2}$, there are two m_I-values $(+\frac{1}{2}$ and $-\frac{1}{2})$ (Figure 4). Thus, if these nuclei are immersed in an external

5

magnetic field, they can only be regarded as being effectively lined up with the field ($m_I = +\frac{1}{2}$) or against the field ($mI = -\frac{1}{2}$). As with compass needless in the Earth's magnetic field, the more favourable energy state is the one corresponding to alignment with the field. The energy difference between the states ΔE is found to be proportional to the strength of the applied field $\mathbf{B_0}$ at the nucleus; actually, ΔE is equal to $\gamma \hbar \mathbf{B_0}$ (Figure 4).

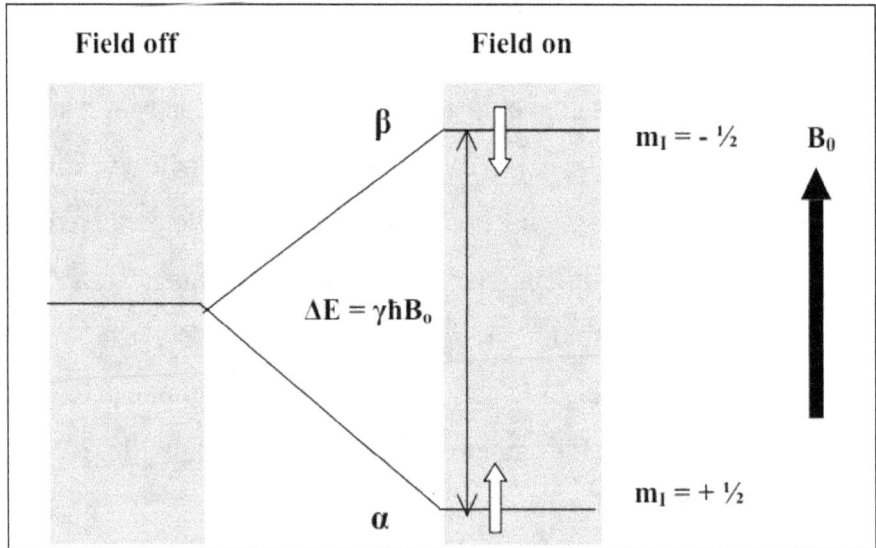

Figure 4: The nuclear spin energy levels of a spin-$\frac{1}{2}$ nucleus in a magnetic field

To observe a nuclear magnetic absorption, we have to adjust either the frequency v_0 of the radiation or the strength of the magnetic field at the nucleus, $\mathbf{B_0}$ until equation (ii) holds, i.e. until the point where resonance (energy absorption) occurs.

The Screening Constant

6

In general, a nucleus is not bare but it is surrounding by electrons. Since electrons are moving charges, they obey to the laws of electromagnetic induction. So, the applied magnetic field, B0, induces circulation in the electron cloud surrounding the nucleus such that, following Lenz' s law, a secondary magnetic field, B´, opposed to B0, is produced (Figure 5)

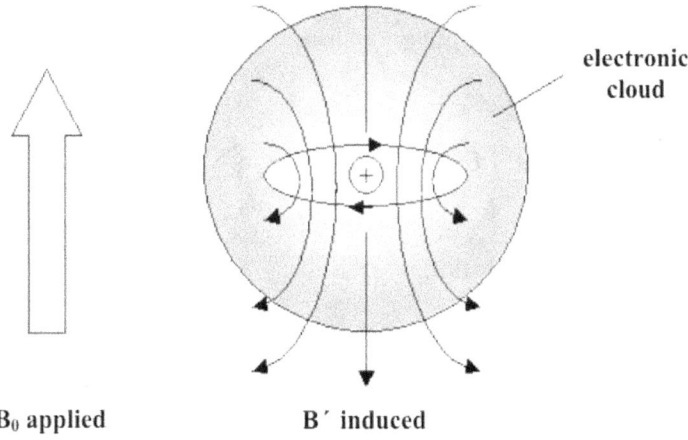

B₀ applied   **B´ induced**

Figure 5: An applied magnetic field $\mathbf{B_0}$ causes the electrons in an atom to circulate within their orbitals. This motion generates an extra field $\mathbf{B´}$ at the nucleus opposing the $\mathbf{B_0}$.

Thus, the local magnetic field that a nucleus experiences, is smaller than the applied field. The nucleus is shielded from the external field by its surrounding electrons by an amount equal to $\mathbf{\sigma B_0}$ where σ is known as the shielding or screening constant, which is a dimensionless quantity:

$$\mathbf{B_{local}} = \mathbf{B_o}\,(1-\sigma) \qquad \dots\dots\dots\dots\dots\text{(vi)}$$

This magnetic shielding has the effect that a higher external field is required to meet the resonance condition in an experiment in which the field is varied, while at a constant field, $\mathbf{B_0}$, the resonance condition is met at a lower frequency than might be expected.

Interpreting ^{1}H NMR Spectra

Information from ^{1}H-NMR spectra:

 a. Number of signals: How many different types of hydrogen's in the molecule

 b. Position of signals (chemical shift): What types of hydrogen's

 c. Relative areas under signals (integration): How many hydrogen's of each type

 d. Splitting pattern: How many neighboring hydrogen's

 1. **Number of signals**: How many different types of hydrogen are in the molecule.

The number of signals will give an indication of the number of different types of hydrogen's that are present. Protons in the same environment are chemically equivalent and will resonate at the same applied strength. Those in a different environment will require a different applied field and therefore will appear at a different position in the spectrum.

8

Examples:

- CH - 1 signal, all H's are in the same environment.

- CH_3CH_3 - 1 signal, all H's are in the same environment.

- $CH_3CH_2CH_3$ - 2 signals, the two sets of CH_3 hydrogens are in the same environment, but are different from the CH_2 hydrogens.

- CH_3-C=O OCH_3 - 2 signals, the two CH_3 groups are in different environments. One is attached to the C=O, and the other is attached to oxygen.

Magnetically equivalent hydrogens resonate at the same applied field.

Magnetically equivalent hydrogens are also chemically equivalent.

one

one

one

two

2.Position of signals (chemical shift): What types of hydrogen's

The shift (chemical shift) is the exact place on the chart where the nucleus absorbs. Shifts are measured in parts per million (ppm), i.e., a percentage of the applied magnetic field. A typical ^{1}H NMR scale is from 0 to 14 ppm, and in most cases, an internal standard (Tetramethylsilane, TMS) is added and is used as the zero reference point. The chemical shift is dependent on the environment (what neighboring nuclei are present) of the hydrogen(s) in question. The nucleus of the hydrogen atom is shielded by the electron that is present, and the neighboring nuclei can either reinforce this shielding or oppose this shielding (deshielding). If the shielding is reinforced, a higher applied magnetic field is needed and the resonance will appear at lower ppm (upfield). If an electronegative element (halogen, oxygen), or an electron withdrawing group (C=O, Ar, C=C) is adjacent, then the shielding is lessened (deshielding occurs) and the resonance will appear at higher ppm (downfield).

primary	0.9 ppm	
secondary	1.3	
tertiary	1.5	
aromatic	6-8.5	
allyl	1.7	
benzyl	2.2-3	
chlorides	3-4	H-C-Cl
bromides	2.5-4	H-C-Br
iodides	2-4	H-C-I
alcohols	3.4-4	H-C-O
alcohols	1-5.5	H-O- (variable)

CH_3CH_2OH has 3 signals:

- one for H's of CH_3 @ between 1 and 1.5 ppm

- one for H's of CH_2 (next to oxygen-deshielded) @ ~3.5 ppm

- one for H of OH (attached directly to oxygen; slightly different

- influence) @ 1 - 4 ppm (actually 4 ppm in this case)

11

Reference compound: Tetramethylsilane (TMS) In order to standardize the NMR spectra, the chemical shifts are positioned in relation to a reference proton set at 0.00 ppm.

Tetramethylsilane, (CH3)4Si, is the standard for ^{1}H NMR. TMS is practical as a reference compound because of its inert quality that prevents it from reacting with the sample and its highly volatile nature that makes it easy to evaporate out of samples. Few compounds have a lower frequency reading than TMS and it has 12 equivalent protons that read strongly on the NMR spectra.

What influences a chemical shift?

Shielding effects: Under an applied magnetic field, circulating electrons in the electron cloud produce a small opposing magnetic field, ultimately decreasing the effective magnetic field felt by the proton, shifting the signal to the right (or upfield). This effect, in which the electron cloud "shields" the proton from the applied magnetic field, is called local diamagnetic shielding.

Electronegativity and deshielding: H's that are attached to more electronegative atoms experience higher chemical shifts. Electronegative atoms also remove electrons from the electron cloud, which decreases their density and results in less shielding; hence electronegative atoms are said to deshield the proton and cause it to have a higher chemical shift, moving it to the left (or downfield). The magnitude of the deshielding effect, however, rapidly decreases as the distance between the proton and electronegative atom increases.

Example: Literature values of the methyl chemical shift as it moves away from bromine

CH_3Br	CH_3CH_2Br	$CH_3CH_2CH_2Br$	$CH_3CH_2CH_2CH_2Br$
269 ppm ppm	1.66 ppm	1.06 ppm	0.93

Magnetic Anisotropy (system ring currents): In molecules containing orbitals, anisotropy (having a different effect along different axes) is responsible for different shielding effects on a proton relative to the applied magnetic field since-orbitals aren't spherically symmetrical.

Intensity of Signal: Integration of Peak Area Integration (relative areas under each signal): how many hydrogen's of each type.

This area is proportional to the number of H's that are responsible for that signal. It will provide a relative ratio of each type of hydrogen that is present in the molecule. Let the smallest integral be 1 and measure all others relative to this. In the event of a 1/2 fraction, multiply all by 2, since ratio should be whole numbers, i.e., a 1:1.5 ratio is 2:3. In the case of the ethanol molecule, integration would show a ratio of 1:2:3.

```
 a   b   c
CH₃CH₂CH₂Br          a    3H          a : b : c = 3 : 2 : 2
                     b    2H
                     c    2H


 a   b   a
CH₃CHCH₃             a    6H          a : b = 6 : 1
     Cl              b    1H
```

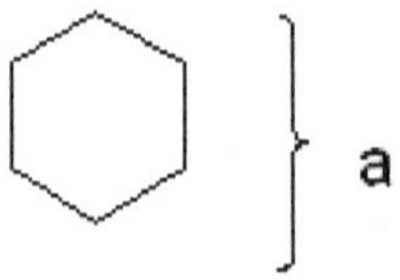

a 12 H

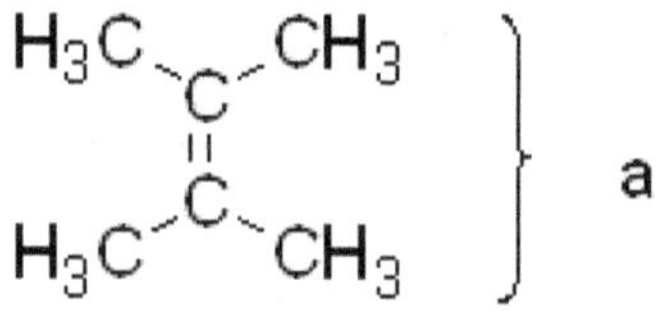

a 12 H

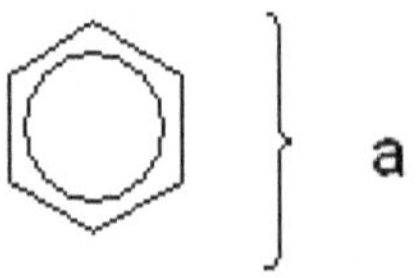

a 6 H

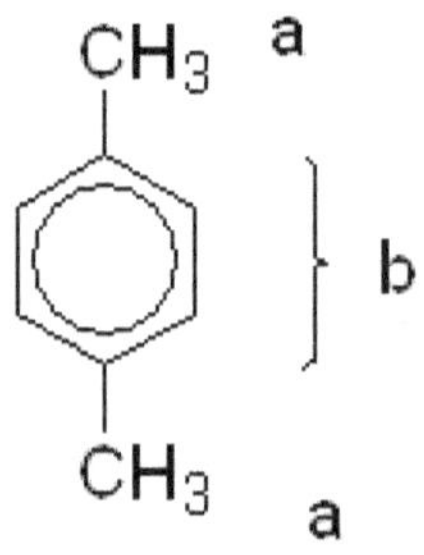

a 6 H
b 4 H

14

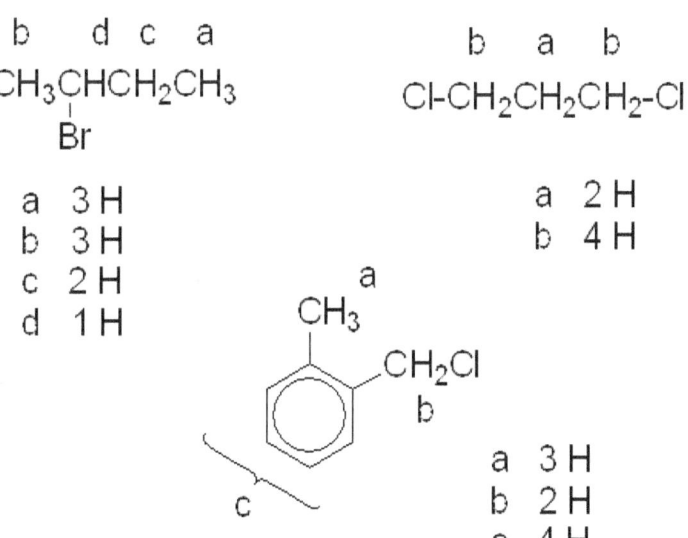

$$\underset{a}{CH_3}$$
$$\underset{a}{H_3C}-\underset{Br}{\overset{|}{C}}-\underset{a}{CH_3}$$

a 9 H

a   b
$$CH_3CH_2\text{-}Br$$

a   3 H
b   2 H

a   b   c
$$CH_3CH_2CH_2\text{-}Br$$

a   3 H
b   2 H
c   2 H

a   b   a
$$CH_3\underset{Cl}{\overset{|}{C}}HCH_3$$

a   6 H
b   1 H

b   d   c   a
$$CH_3\underset{Br}{\overset{|}{C}}HCH_2CH_3$$

a   3 H
b   3 H
c   2 H
d   1 H

b   a   b
$$Cl\text{-}CH_2CH_2CH_2\text{-}Cl$$

a   2 H
b   4 H

a
CH_3
CH_2Cl
b

c

a   3 H
b   2 H
c   4 H

3. Splitting pattern: Splitting of the Signal into Several Peaks: Spin-Spin Splitting: How many neighboring hydrogen's

This is a powerful tool in deducing the ^{1}HNMR spectra. The neighboring hydrogen nuclei will cause the signal to split. Two things one should consider when examining spin-spin splitting are: Chemically equivalent hydrogen nuclei do not cause splitting to occur, whether they are on the same carbon or a different one.

$$
\begin{array}{c}
H \\
| \\
H - C - H \\
| \\
Cl
\end{array}
$$

.

Figure 1: All three H's are equilvalent; therefore, no splitting

$$
\begin{array}{cc}
H & H \\
| & | \\
H - C - C - H \\
| & | \\
H & H
\end{array}
$$

Figure 2: All 6 H's are chemically equilvalent; therefore, no splitting

In general, n-equivalent neighboring hydrogens will split a ^{1}H signal into an (n + 1) peaks Pascal pattern.

16

n	n − 1	Pascal pattern:	
0	1	1	singlet
1	2	1 1	doublet
2	3	1 2 1	triplet
3	4	1 3 3 1	quartet
4	5	1 4 6 4 1	quintet

The distance between the split peaks are called coupling constants, denoted by J. The interaction between nearby protons produce different spin flip energies as they can orient themselves in a pattern of parallel or antiparallel to the applied magnetic force. This phenomenon, where the spin of the nucleus of one proton is close enough to affect the spin of another, is called spin-spin coupling. Splitting is always reciprocated between the protons—if Ha splits Hb, then Hb must split Ha—and provides information on the neighbors of a proton within the molecule.

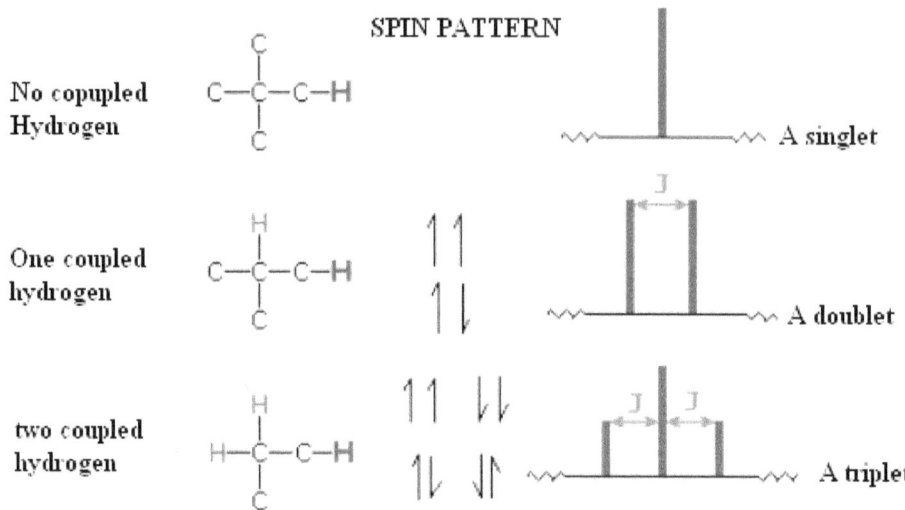

1 neighbor → doublet; 2 neighbors → triplet; 3 neighbors → quartet .

Splitting patterns that are too difficult to analyze are called multiplet

Rules/Restrictions for Proton coupling

1. Nuclei with the same chemical shift (isochronous) do not couple with each other: the protons must be nonequivalent in order to couple.

2. Vicinal protons (protons separated by 3 bonds) can couple with each other. Protons that are more than 3 bonds away cannot because the signal they feel from their neighbor is too small to affect their spin. There is also geminal coupling-coupling through 2 bonds) and allylic coupling—coupling through1 4 bonds, if one is a pi bond. Pi bonds do not follow the 3 bond rule because the electron density around a pi bond is higher than in a single bond; hence, pi bonds can be counted as a free spacer. All hydrogens on the benzene ring couple with each other and the ring itself can be counted as a free spacer;

18

however, H's on the benzene ring only couple with each other and not with H's attached to other atoms even if they are within the 3 bond max limit.

2. Hydrogens bonded to a Nitrogen or Oxygen usually do not couple with other protons and appear as singlet on the NMR spectra.

Non-first order splitting: the N+1 rule cannot predict the exact splitting patterns of non-first order splitting. First order splitting produces "normal" splitting patterns that have equal J values. Non-first order splitting occurs when a nucleus spin-couples with 2 or more sets of nearby nuclei that have different J values.

Example of First Order Splitting and Non-First Order

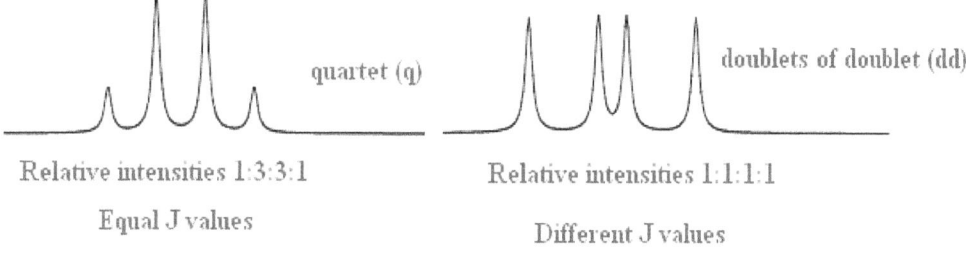

quartet (q)

Relative intensities 1:3:3:1

Equal J values

doublets of doublet (dd)

Relative intensities 1:1:1:1

Different J values

2nd Order Coupling Effects

First order theory is sufficient when describing NMR signals of coupled nuclei that are far enough apart from each other; however, when the chemical shifts come closer, other effects (second order coupling effects) begin to take over. Two things occur as a result of

19

these weaker interactions: spin state energies shift and the intensities of the peak change and no longer adhere to the pascal triangle pattern.

Hydrogen a and b are both doublet of doublets due to 2nd order coupling effects.

RULES FOR SPECTRAL ANALYSIS OF FIRST ORDER SPECTRA

Rule 1: A group of n magnetically equivalent protons will split a resonance of an interacting group of protons into $n+I$ lines. For example, the resonance due to the A protons in an *AnXm*system will be split into $m+I$ lines, while the resonance due to the X protons will be split into $n+1$ lines. More generally, splitting by n nuclei of spin quantum number I, results in $2nI+$ I lines. This simply reduces to $n+I$ for protons where $I = Yz$.

Rule 2: The spacing (measured in Hz) of the lines in the multiplet will be equal to the coupling constant. In the above example all spacings in both parts of the spectrum will be equal to *JAX*

Rule 3: The true chemical shift of each group of interacting protons lies in the centre of the (always symmetrical) multiplet.

Rule 4: The relative intensities of the lines within each multiplet will be in the ratio of the binomial coefficients. In the case of higher multiplets, the outside components of multiplets are relatively weak and may be lost in the instrumental noise, *e.g.* a septet may appear as a quintet if the outer lines are not clearly visible. The intensity relationship is the first to be significantly distorted in non-ideal cases, but this does not lead to serious errors in spectral analysis.

Rule 5: When a group of magnetically equivalent protons interacts with more than one group of protons, its resonance will take the form of a multiplet of multiplets. For example, the resonance due to the A protons in a system AnM~m will have the multiplicity of *(p+I)(m+ I)*. The multiplet patterns are chained *e.g.* a proton coupled to 2 different protons will be split to a doublet by coupling to the first proton then each of the component of the doublet will be split further by coupling to the second proton resulting in a symmetrical multiplet with 4 lines (a doublet of doublets)

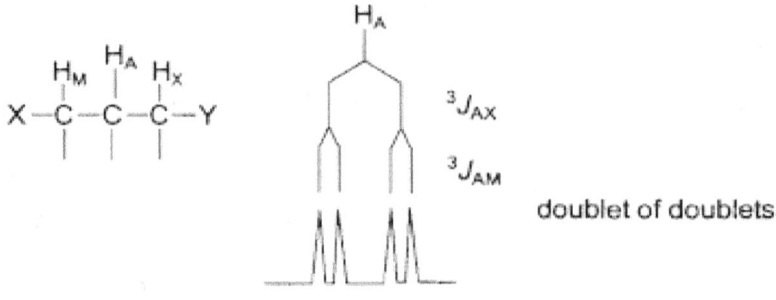

doublet of doublets

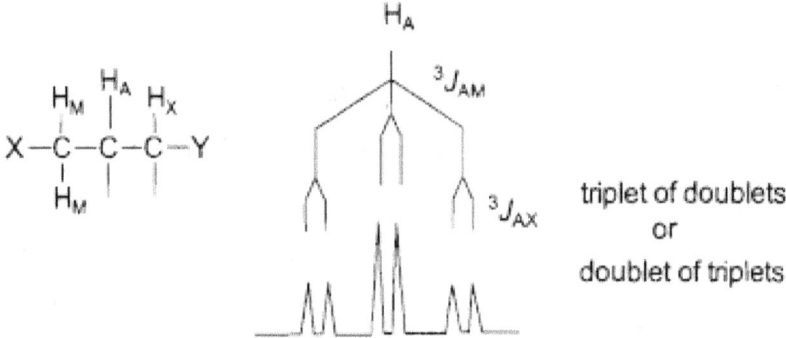

triplet of doublets

or

doublet of triplets

The appropriate coupling constants will control splitting and relative intensities will obey rule 4.

Rule 6: Protons that are magnetically equivalent do not split each other. Any system A_n will give rise to a singlet.

Rule 7: Spin systems that contain groups of chemically equivalent protons that are not magnetically equivalent cannot be analyzed by first-order methods.

Rule 8: If $\Delta V_{AB}/J_{AB}$ is less than -3, for any pair of nuclei A and B in the spin system, the spectra become distorted from the expected ideal multiplet patterns and the spectra cannot be analyzed by first-order methods.

NUCLEAR RESONANCE

In NMR experiment, a strong homogeneous magnetic field is applied causing the nuclei to precess. Radiation of energy comparable to ΔE is then imposed with a radiofrequency source. When the applied frequency from the radiofrequency sources becomes equals to the Larmour frequency or angular frequency of precession, the two are said to be in resonance. Due to this resonance some nuclei are excited from the low energy state (m=-1/2) to higher energy state (m=+1/2) by the absorption of energy E from the sources a frequency equal to to Larmour frequency. If the magnetic field of radiation is oscillating in plane at right angle to the applied field and frequency of radiation is same as the Larmour frequency of precession of the nuclei then the transfer of energy from the radiation to the nuclei will occur leading to the phenomenon of resonance.

SATURATION

When a nucleus is exposed to radiation of suitable frequency, absorption takes place due to slight excess of lower energy state nuclei that are present in the strong magnetic field. This excess is small and so there is always a possibility that the absorption process

23

will equalize the number of nuclei in the two states. This causes the absorption signal to decrease and to approach zero. Under this condition the spin system is said to be saturated and the process is called saturation. In order to prevent saturation, the rate of relaxation of excited nuclei to their lowest energy state must be greater than the rate at which they absorb the radio frequency energy. To reduce saturation and to produce a readily detectable absorption signal, relaxation is expected to occur as readily as possible.

RELAXATION PROCESS

Relaxation processes involves non-radiative transitions by which a nucleus in upper transition state returns to the lower spin state. There are two types of relaxation process:

1. Spin-Spin Relaxation: (Transverse Relaxation)

This is affected by the mutual exchange of spins by two precesseing nucleus in the close proximity to one another. With each precessing nucleus, there is an associated magnetic field vector component rotating in a plane perpendicular to the main field. If this small rotating magnetic field is same as is required to induce a transition in the neighbouring proton, then mutual exchange of spin takes place. This mutual exchange of spins shortens the life time of an individual nucleus in the higher energy state. In other words, it involves the transfer of energy from one nucleus to the other. There is no net loss of energy. The spread of energy among the nuclei concerned results in line broadening.

24

2. Spin-Lattice Relaxation (Longitudinal Relaxation)

The term lattice refers to the frame work of molecules containing the prcessing nuclei. All these molecules undergo translational, vibrational and rotational motion and possess magnetic properties, giving rise to small magnetic fields in the lattice. A properly oriented small magnetic field induces a transition in a particular precessing magnet from an upper state to the lower state. The energy from this transition is transferred to the components of the lattice a additional translational and vibrational energy. This maintains the excess of nuclei in the lower energy state. An efficient relaxation process involves a short time and results in the broadening of absorption peaks. Smaller the time of the excited sate, grater is the line width.

SHIELDING AND DESHIELDING EFFECTS

Hydrogen nuclei in a molecule are surrounded by the electronic charge which shields the nucleus from the influence of the applie field. So to overcome the shielding effect and to bring the protons to resonance, greater external field is required. Evidently greater the electron de3nsity around the proton, greater will be the induced secondary magnetic field which opposes the applied field. Hence greater external field will cause proton absorption. The extent of shielding is shown in terms of shielding parameter, α. When absorption occurs, the field H feld by the proton is represented as

$H = H_0 (1 - \alpha.)$…………..(i)

Where H_0 is the applied field strength

However the field felt by the proton does not correspond to the applied field. Greater the value of α., greater will be the value of applied field strength which has to be applied to get the effective field required for absorption and vica versa.

Also $$\upsilon = \gamma H_0/2\pi \ldots \ldots \ldots \ldots \ldots (ii)$$

So we have

$$\upsilon = (1-\alpha)\, \gamma H_0/2\pi \ldots \ldots \ldots \ldots (iii)$$

so it is clear that the proton with different electronic environments or with different shielding parameter can be brought into resonance in two ways:

- The strength of external field is kept steady and the radiofrequency is constantly varied and
- The radiofrequency is kept steady and the strength of the applied field is constantly varied.

EXERCISES WITH SOLUTION

Que 1: Analyze the proton magnetic resonance spectrum of diethylketone

Ans

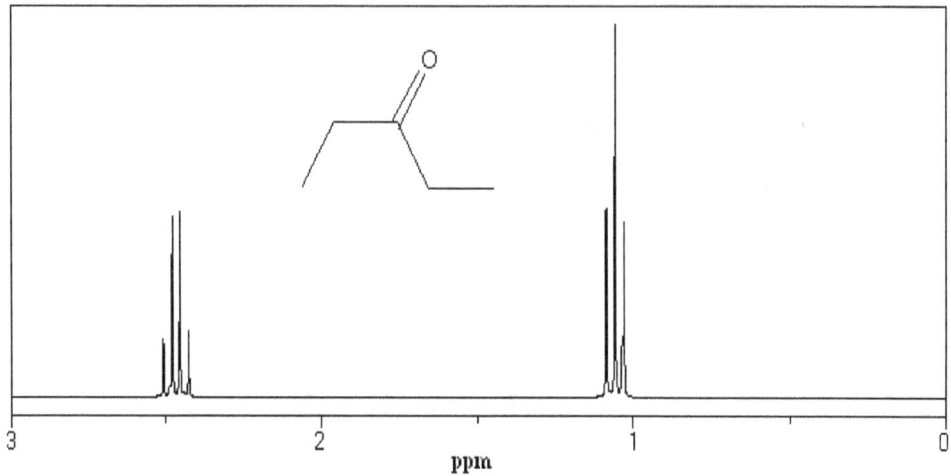

Each CH$_2$ group is split by the neighboring CH$_3$ group into a 1:3:3:1 quartet. Correspondingly, each CH$_3$ group is split by the neighboring CH$_2$

into a 1:2:1 triplet. So we find 3H doublet and 2 H quartet.

Que 2: The NMR spectrum of methane CH$_4$ shows just a single peak. Explain, why.

Ans: The protons in methane are equivalent and do not exhibit spin-spin splitting.

Que 3: The proton magnetic resonance spectrum of toluene shows two peaks with relative intensities 5 : 3. Explain this spectrum.

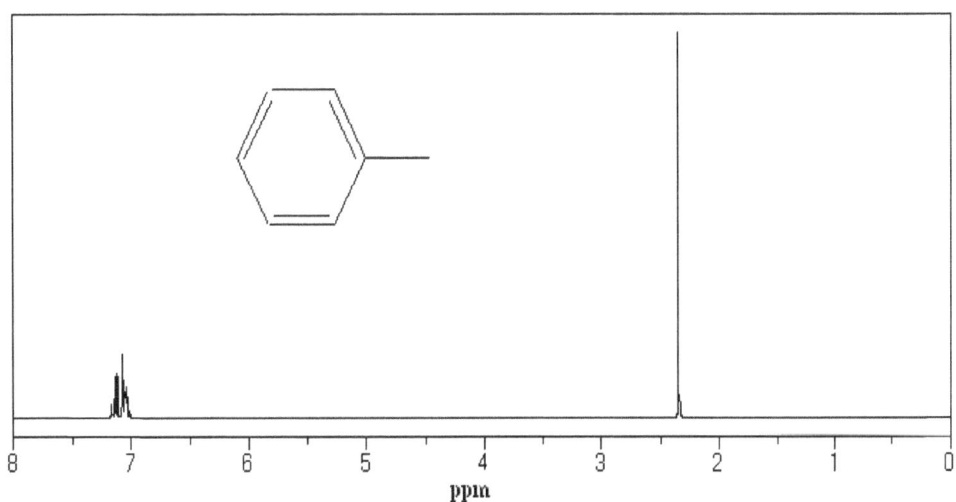

The 3 protons in the methyl group are equivalent with a chemical shift $\delta \approx 2$. The 5 protons on the phenyl group are not strictly equivalent but, evidently, their chemical shifts are nearly equal.

Que 4: Analyze the proton magnetic resonance spectrum of 1,1-dibromoethane.

The bromine nuclei do not cause any detectable splittings. The methyl protons are split into a doublet by the alone proton on the other carbon atom. The latter proton is itself split into a 1:3:3:1 quartet.

29

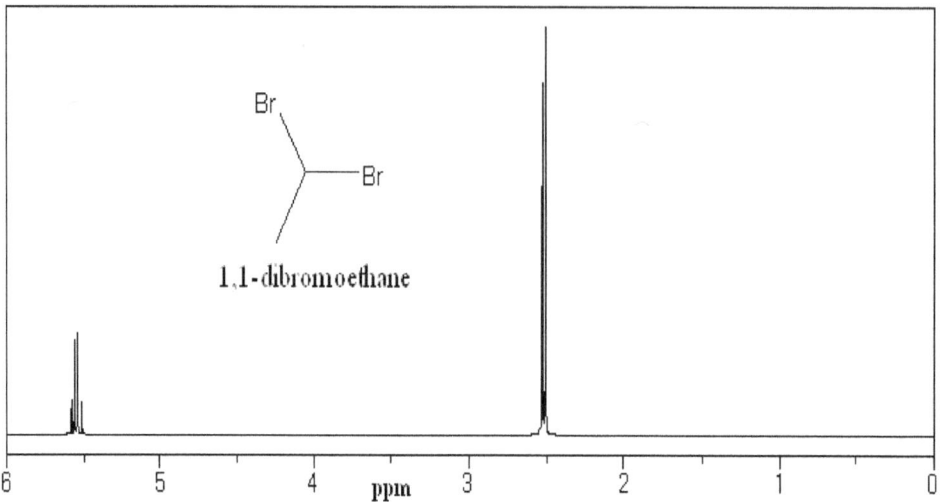

1,1-dibromoethane

Que5: For the following compounds indicate the number of signals that would appear in its proton NMR spectrum.

Ans: There is local symmetry among the three methyl hydrogens at site a; therefore, they are chemically equivalent to one another. There is local symmetry among the three methyl hydrogens at site b; therefore, they are chemically equivalent to one another.

30

Considering the way the molecule is drawn, the top half of the molecule is not the mirror image of the bottom half (specifically, the bromine above the barrier is not the reflection of the hydrogen below the barrier); thus methyl group (a) and methyl group (b) are not equivalent. The double bond is a barrier to free rotation, there is no free rotation around it. Methyl group a is permanently fixed on the same side of the double bond as the bromine; thus it experiences a different environment than methyl group b, which is permanently fixed on the same side of the double bond as hydrogen c. So there will be three signals in the 1H NMR spectrum of 1-bromo-2-methylprop-1-ene.

Que 6: For the following compound indicates the number of signals that would appear in its proton NMR spectrum.

$$CH_3CCl_3$$

Ans: At the methyl group (site a.), because there is free rotation about the C_a-CCl_3 bond, the three hydrogens experience the same environment and are therefore said to be chemically equivalent to one another.

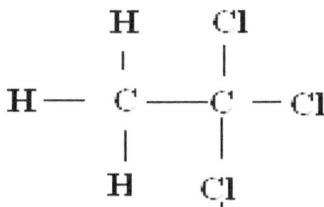

Considering the way the molecule is drawn, there is a horizontal mirror plane of symmetry in the molecule such that the top half of the molecule is a reflection of the bottom half. This symmetry also contributes to the chemical equivalence among the methyl hydrogens. One NMR signal will represent all three hydrogens

Que 7: For the cyclopropane indicates the number of signals that would appear in its proton NMR spectrum.

Ans. Through the methylene carbon 1 and the C_2-C_3 bond there is a vertical mirror plane of symmetry in the molecule, such that the left side of the molecule is a reflection of the right side; because of this symmetry,

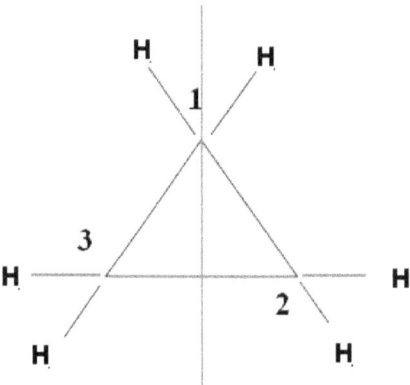

the two hydrogens on C_1 are equivalent to one another. The two hydrogens at C_3 are a reflection of the two hydrogens at C_2; therefore, these four hydrogens are equivalent to one another. Use your skills of visualization to see there is a diagonal mirror plane through the methylene carbon 2 and the C_1-C_3 bond, and another diagonal mirror plane through the methylene carbon 3 and the C_1-C_2 bond, therefore, all six hydrogens in cyclopropane are chemically equivalent to one another and will be represented by the same NMR signal.

There will be one signal in the proton NMR spectrum of this compound.

Que 8:For the following compound indicate the number of signals that would appear in its proton NMR spectrum.

$$CH_3\!\!-\!\!CH\!-\!CH_2\!\!-\!\!I$$
$$|$$
$$OD$$

Ans

At the methylene groups, (a) there is free rotation about the Ca-Cb bond; this creates "local symmetry"; therefore, the two hydrogen's of group a. are equivalent to one another. The hydrogen attached to the oxygen is a deuterium atom and is therefore NMR inactive (has no 1HNMR signal). The hydrogen at (b) gives one NMR signal. There is free rotation about the C_b-C_c bond; this creates "local symmetry"; therefore, the three hydrogen's of group (c). are equivalent to one

33

another. There will be three signals in the proton NMR spectrum of this compound.

Que 9: For the following compound indicates the number of signals that would appear in its proton NMR spectrum.

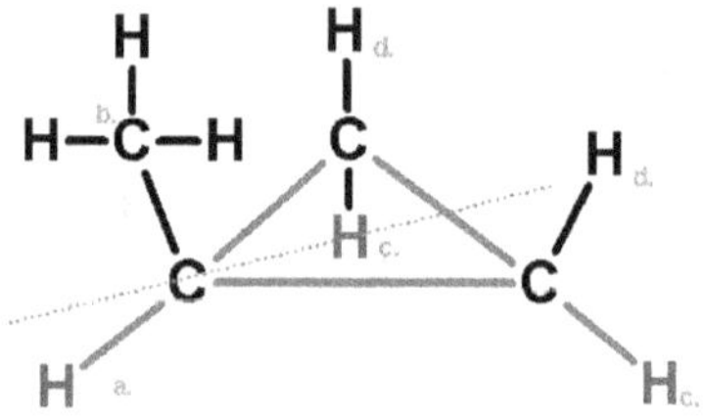

In the model shown above, those atoms/substituent's which are above the plane of ring are black, those which are below the ring are blue. Through carbon 1 (which has hydrogen a and the methyl group attached to it) and the C_2-C_3 bond there is a vertical mirror plane of symmetry (represented by the dashed red line) in the molecule, such that the front of the molecule is a reflection of the back; because of this symmetry, the two hydrogens above the plane, labeled d, are equivalent to one another and the two hydrogens below the plane, labeled c, are equivalent to one another.

There will be four signals (Ha, Hb, Hc, and Hd) in the proton NMR spectrum of this compound.

Que 10: For the following compound indicates the number of signals that would appear in its proton NMR spectrum.

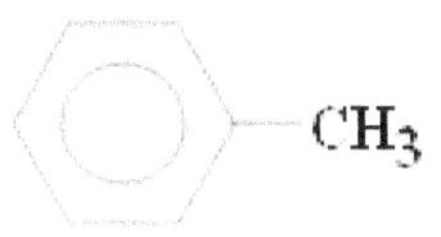

Ans

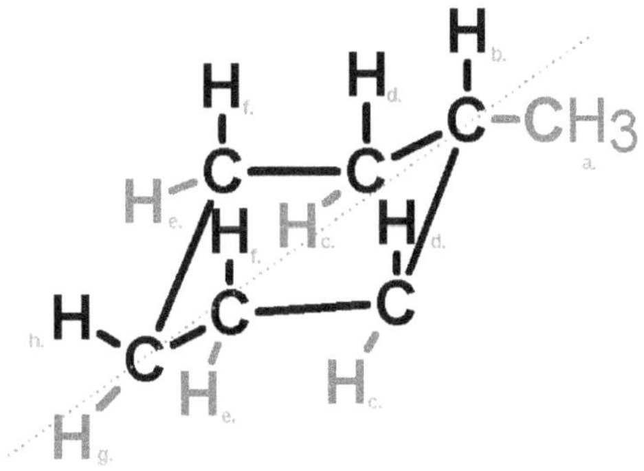

In the model shown above, those atoms/substituent's which are above the ring are black; those which are below the ring are blue. Through ring carbon 1 (which has hydrogen b. and the methyl group a. attached to it) and ring carbon 4 (which has hydrogens g and h attached to it) there is a vertical mirror plane of symmetry (represented by the dashed red line) in the molecule, such that the front of the molecule is a reflection of the back. Because of this symmetry, the two hydrogens above the plane, labeled d, are equivalent to one another, the two hydrogens below the plane, labeled c, are equivalent to one another, the two hydrogens above the plane,

35

labeled f, are equivalent to one another, the two hydrogens below the plane, labeled e, are equivalent to one another.

There will be eight signals in the proton NMR spectrum of this compound.

Que11: For the following compound indicates the number of signals that would appear in its proton NMR spectrum.

$$BrCH_2CH_2CH_2Br$$

Ans

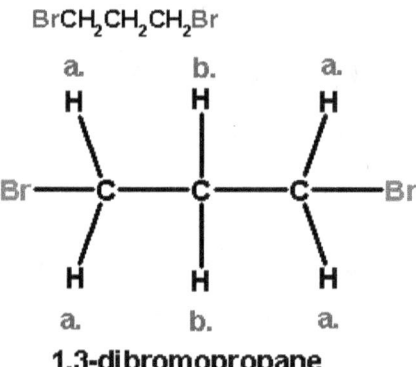

1,3-dibromopropane

At the methylene groups, a, there is free rotation about the C_a-C_b bond; therefore the two hydrogens of the left hand methylene group, a, are equivalent to one another. Another reason for the chemical equivalence of these two hydrogens is the symmetry in the molecule; a horizontal mirror plane goes through the carbon skeleton such that the top of the molecule is a reflection of the bottom of the molecule.

The two hydrogens of the right hand methylene groups are chemically equivalent to one another for the same reasons as the left hand group.

There is a vertical mirror plane of symmetry in the molecule; it goes through the methylene carbon b such that the left side of the molecule is a reflection of the right side; because of this symmetry, the four methylene hydrogens, labeled a, are equivalent to one another and will be represented by the same NMR signal.

At methylene group b., there is free rotation about the C_b-C_a bonds, and symmetry (the horizontal mirror plane); therefore, the two hydrogens labeled b. are chemically equivalent to one another, and will be represented by the same NMR signal.

There will be two signals in the proton NMR spectrum of this compound

Que12: For the following compound indicates the number of signals that would appear in its proton NMR spectrum.

$$\begin{array}{c} CH_3 \\ | \\ H_3C-C-CH_2 \\ | \quad \backslash \\ H_2C \quad CH_3 \end{array}$$

Ans

$$H_3C-\underset{\underset{\overset{|}{H_2C}}{\overset{|}{|}}}{\overset{\overset{b.}{CH_3}}{\overset{|}{C}}}-CH_2$$

b.
b. CH₃
    |
H₃C–C–CH₂ c.
    |
   H₂C   CH₃ d.
      ＼ Cl
   a.

1-chloro-2,2-dimethylbutane

At the methylene group, a, there is free rotation about the C_a-C_b bond; this creates "local symmetry"; therefore, the two hydrogens are equivalent to one another. Also, the molecule can be drawn in a way that demonstrates a mirror plane of symmetry, such that half of the molecule is a reflection of the other half. Thus, one methylene hydrogen is the reflection of the other methylene hydrogen. This symmetry is another reason for the chemical equivalence of the two methylene hydrogens. Because of free rotation about C-C bonds, local symmetry exist which causes local symmetry, and therefore chemical equivalence within each methyl group labeled b. Also, molecular symmetry causes one methyl group b to be the reflection of the other methyl group b; therefore, the six hydrogens at b give one NMR signal. Free rotation about the C-C bonds causes "local symmetry" at site. C. Also because of molecular symmetry, one methylene hydrogen c is a reflection of the other, therefore, the two hydrogens of group c are equivalent to one another. At methyl group d., there is free rotation about the C_c-C_d bond causing local symmetry, and also molecular symmetry, causing the three hydrogens of group d to be equivalent to one another.

There will be four signals in the proton NMR spectrum of this compound.

Que13: For the following compound indicates the number of signals that would appear in its proton NMR spectrum.

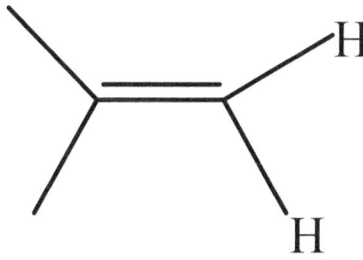

Ans

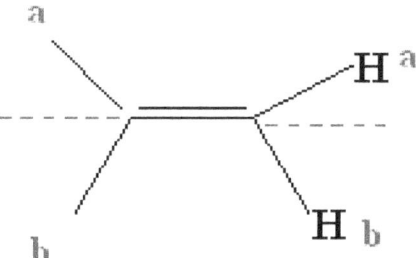

Within each methyl group local symmetry causes chemical equivalence. There is a horizontal mirror plane of symmetry through the molecule, represented by the red dashed line. Because of this symmetry the two methyl groups a are chemically equivalent to one another, and the two methine hydrogens b are chemically equivalent to one another.

There will be two signals in the proton NMR spectrum of this compound (2-methylprop-1-ene).

Que15: For the following compounds indicate the number of signals that would appear in its proton NMR spectrum.

Ans

Within each methyl group local symmetry causes chemical equivalence. Free rotation about the Cb-C=O bond causes local symmetry between the two methyl groups labeled a--on the left side of the molecule, and between the two methyl groups labeled a--on the right side of the molecule. There is a vertical mirror plane of symmetry through the molecule, represented by the red dashed line. This symmetry results in the two methyl groups on the left side of the molecule, being chemically equivalent to the two methyl groups on the right side of the molecule, and the methine hydrogen on the leftside being equivalent to the methine hydrogen on the right.

There will be two signals in the proton NMR spectrum of this compound (1,4-dimethylpentan-3-one).

Que16: For the following compound indicates the number of signals that would appear in its proton NMR spectrum.

$$CH_3\,CO\,C(CH_3)_3$$

Ams: It shows two singles one due to CH_3 group and other singlet due to none equivalents protons of Tert butyl group. So we finds 3H singlet and 9H singlet.

Que 17: For the following compounds indicate the number of signals that would appear in its proton N MR spectrum.

$$CH_3\text{-}CH_2\text{-}CH_2\text{-}CO\text{-}CH_3$$

Ans

1. Singlet signal of three proton due to -CO-CH_3 group (3H singlet)

2. Triplet of two protons due to –CH_2- group attached to –CO- group (2H triplet)

3. Triplet of three protons due to –CH_2 group attached to CH_3- group (3H triplet)

41

4. Multiplet signal is for two protons (2H multiplet)

Que18: For the following compound indicates the number of signals that would appear in its proton N MR spectrum.
$$CH_3\text{--}CO\text{-}NH\text{-}CH_3$$

Ans

1. Three proton singlet due to CH_3- group attached to –CO- group (3H singlet).

2. Three Proton doublet due to another CH_3- group attached to – NH- group (3H Doublet)

3. 1 proton quartet of attached to –CH_3- group (1H quartet)

Que 19: For the following compound indicates the number of signals that would appear in its proton NMR spectrum.

$$C_6H_5\text{-}CH_2\text{-}CH_2\text{-}OCO\text{-}CH_3$$

Ans

1. 3H singlet due to CH_3 attached to –CO- group (3H singlet)

2.2H triplet due to –CH_2- group attached to another –CH_2- group (2H doublet).

3. 5H triplet due to C_6H_5 group.

Que 20: For the following compound indicates the number of signals that would appear in its proton NMR spectrum

$$CH_3CH_2Br$$

3H triplet and 2H Quartet

Que 21: For the t- butyl phenol indicates the number of signals that would appear in its proton NMR spectrum

Ans; There are four types of proton in t-butyl phenol

Two 2H triplet, 9H singlet and 1H of –OH group as singlet

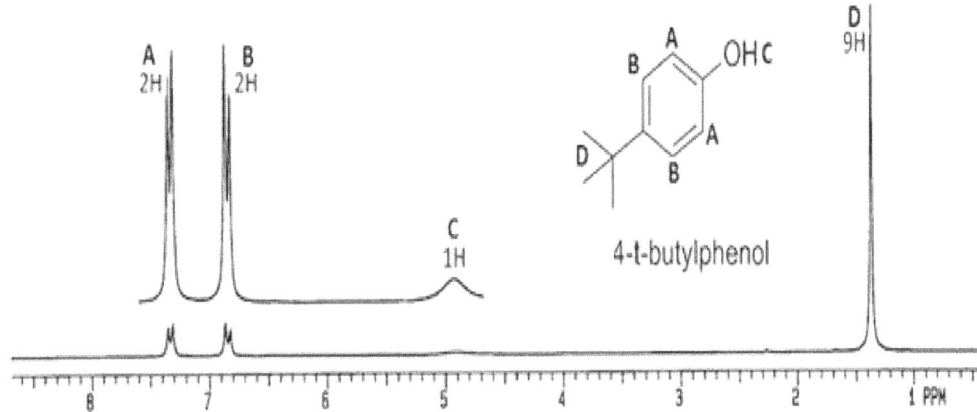

Que 22: For the 2-bromobutane indicates the number of signals that would appear in its proton NMR spectrum.

Ans: There is four types of protons in 2-bromobutane.

No of peaks are: 3H doublet of c- type, 1 H multiplet due to a- type proton, 2H pentet due to b- types of proton and 3H triplet due to d-types of proton.

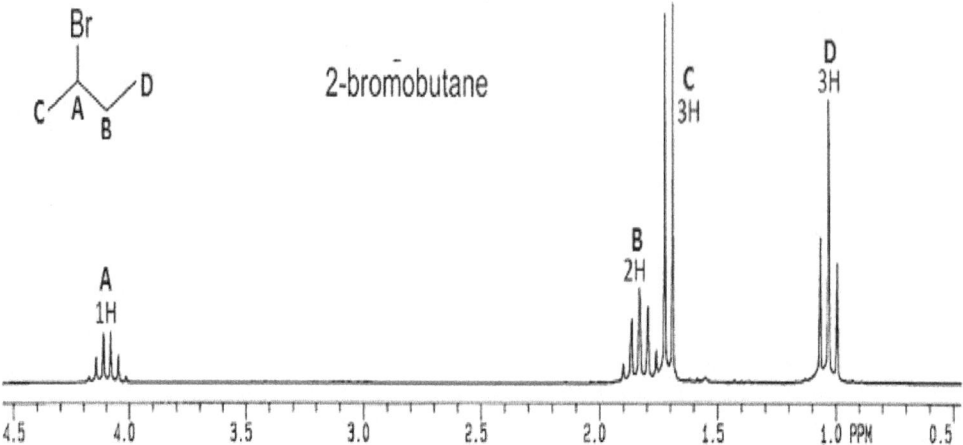

Que 23: For the 1-ethylpropanamine indicates the number of signals that would appear in its proton NMR spectrum.

Ans: There are four types of proton in 1-ethyl propanamine as indicated. Peaks are:

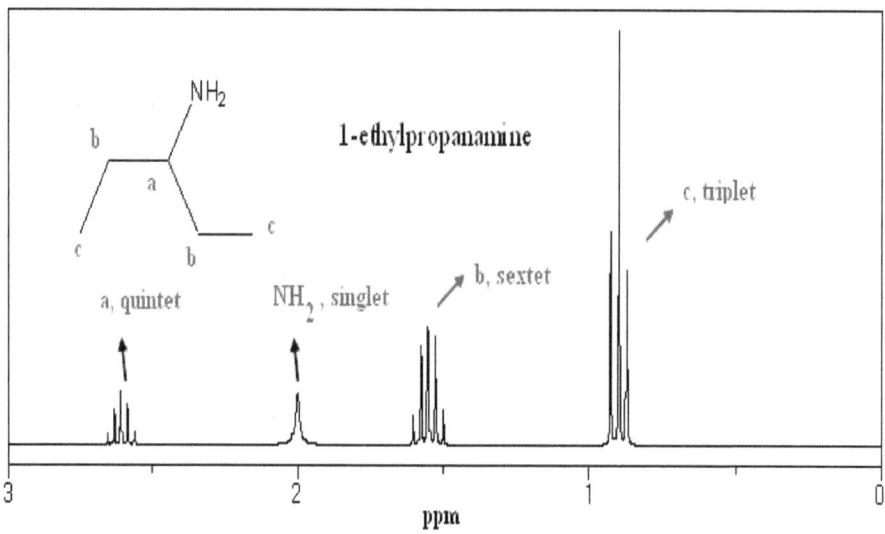

44

Que 24: For the 3-methylbenzoic acid indicates the number of signals that would appear in its proton NMR spectrum

Ans: There are three types of proton in 3-methylbenzoic acid as indicated.

Number of peaks is;

1H singlet, 4H two singlets, 3H singlet

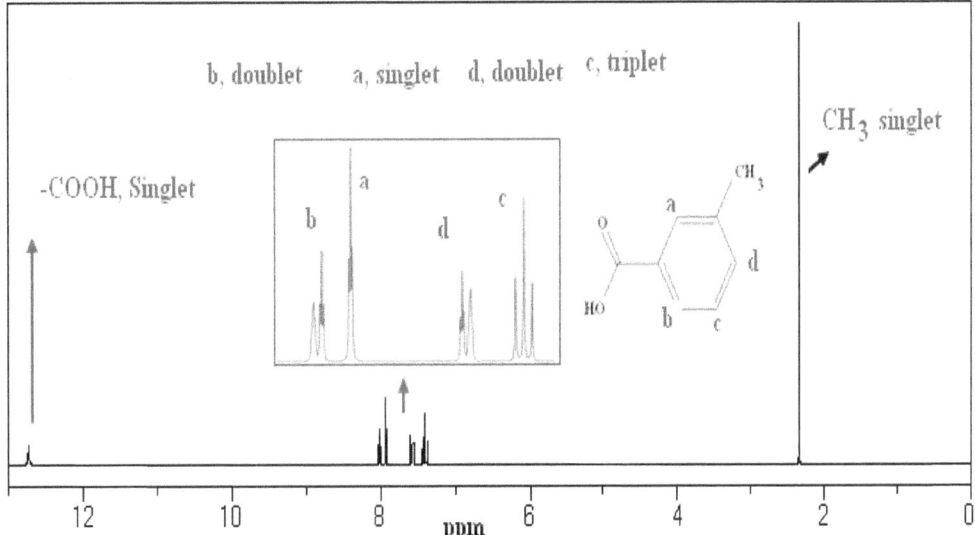

Que 25: For the propanoic acid indicates the number of signals that would appear in its proton NMR spectrum.

Ans. There are three types of protons in propanoic acid as indicated.

Numbers of peaks are: 1H singlet, 2H quartet, and 3H triplet

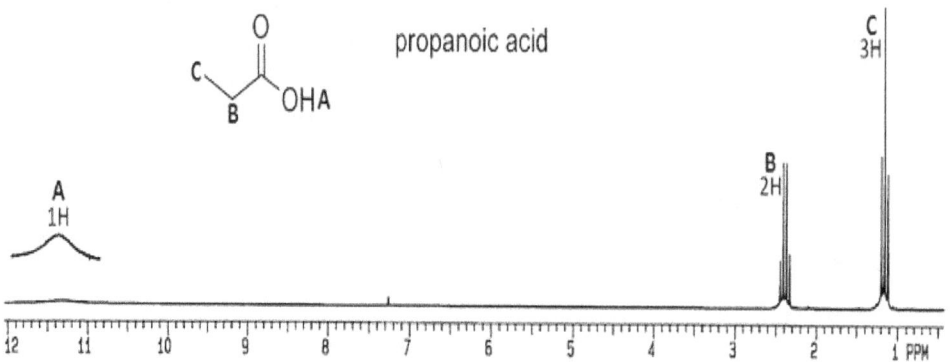

Que 26: For the 4-butylbenzaldehyde indicates the number of signals that would appear in its proton NMR spectrum.

Ans: There are seven types of proton as indicated and numbers of signals are:

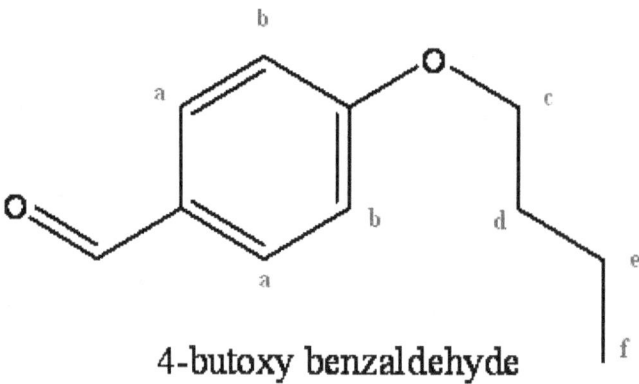

4-butoxy benzaldehyde

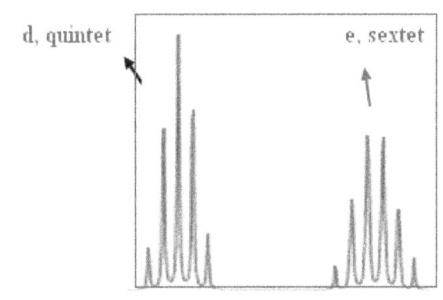

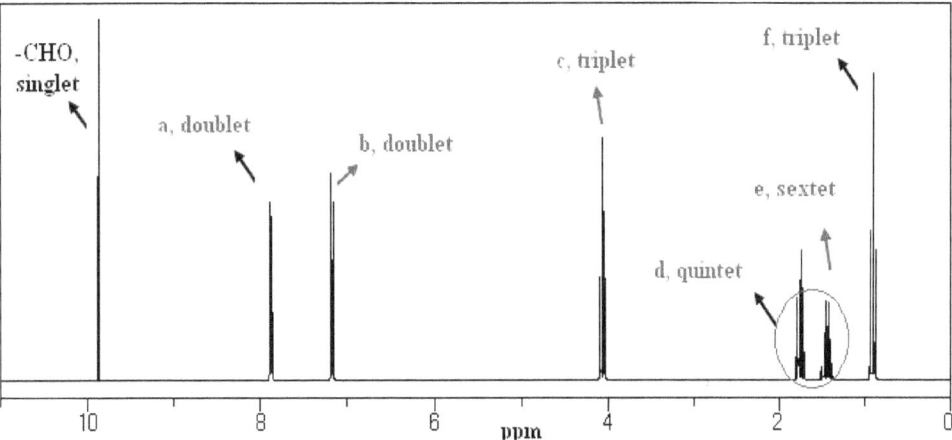

Que 27: For the following compound indicates the number of signals that would appear in its proton NMR spectrum.

$CH_3CH_2CH_2Br$

Ans: There are three types of proton and number of signals is:

2H triplet, 3H triplet, 2H sextet

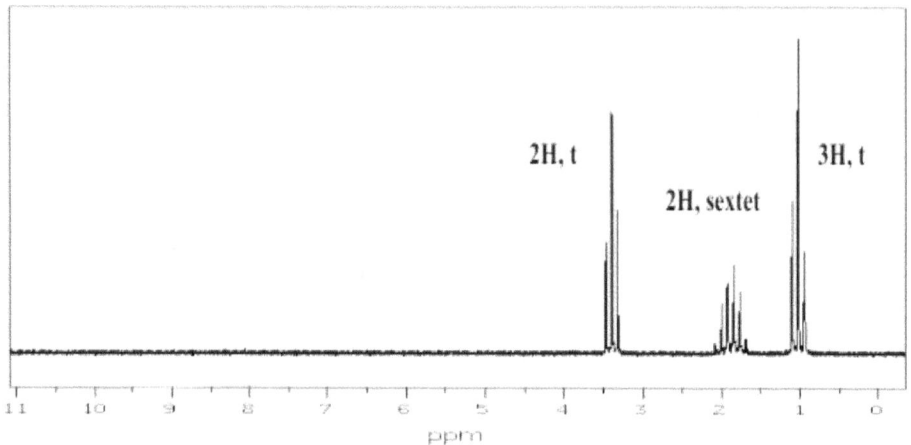

Que 28: For the following compound indicates the number of signals that would appear in its proton NMR spectrum.

$$CH_3CH_2CH_2CH_2CHO$$

Ans; There are five types of protons as indicated and number of peaks are 1H singlet, 2H triplet, 2H pentet, 2H sextet and 3H triplet

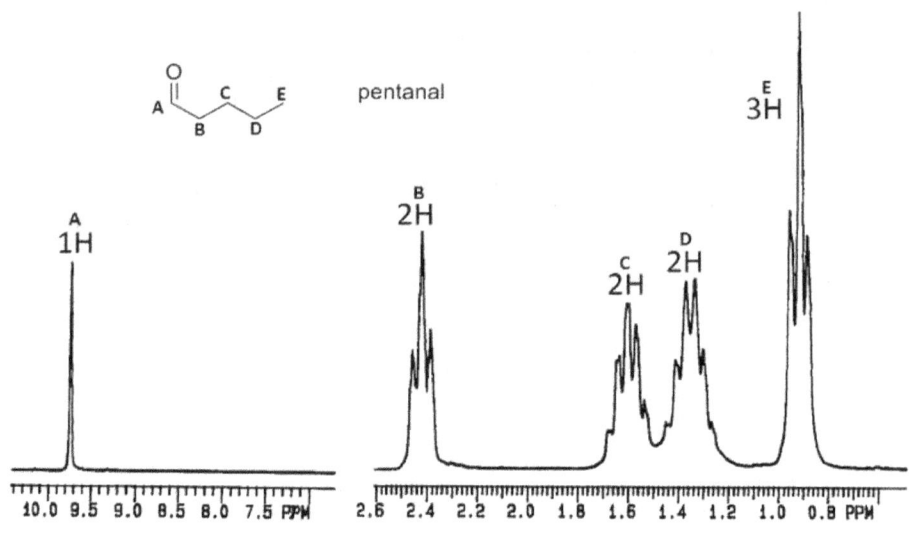

48

Que 29: For the following compound indicates the number of signals that would appear in its proton NMR spectrum

$$H_3C-\underset{\underset{H}{|}}{\overset{\overset{Br}{|}}{C}}-CH_2-CH_3$$

Ans: There are four types of proton and numbers of signals are:

1H sextet, 3H doublet, 3H triplet and 2H pentet

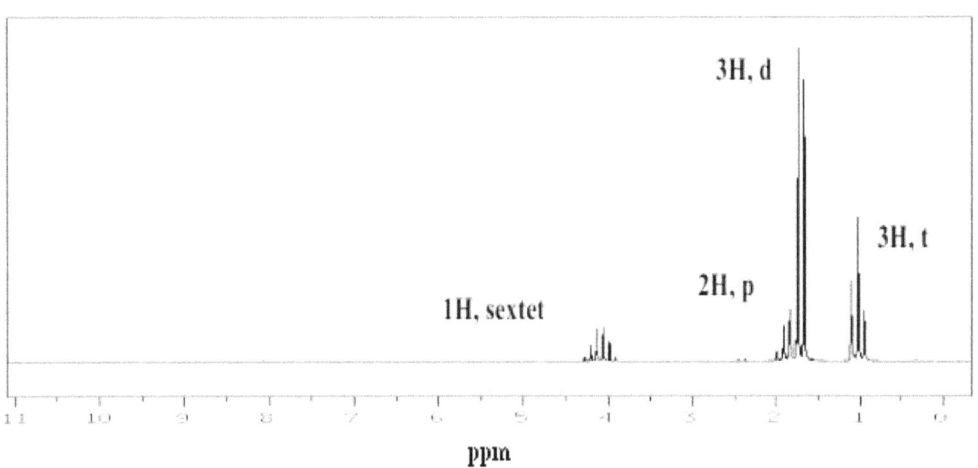

Que 31: For the following compound indicates the number of signals that would appear in its proton NMR spectrum

$$CH_3-\underset{\underset{H}{|}}{\overset{\overset{CH_2Br}{|}}{C}}-CH_3$$

Ans: there are three types of protons and signals are 2H doublet, 6H doublet, 1H multiplet

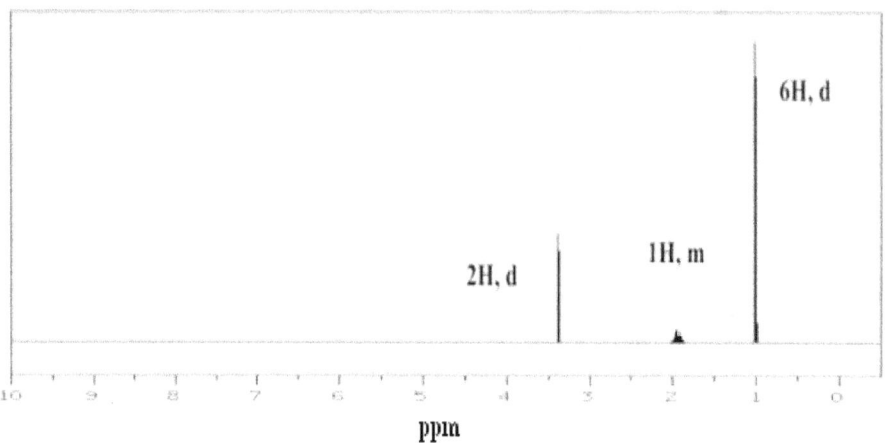

Que 32: For the following compound indicates the number of signals that would appear in its proton NMR spectrum.

ethyl 3-oxohexanoate

Ans: There are six types of protons and numbers of signals are: 2H quartet, 2H singlet, 2H triplet, 2H sextet, two 3H triplet,

50

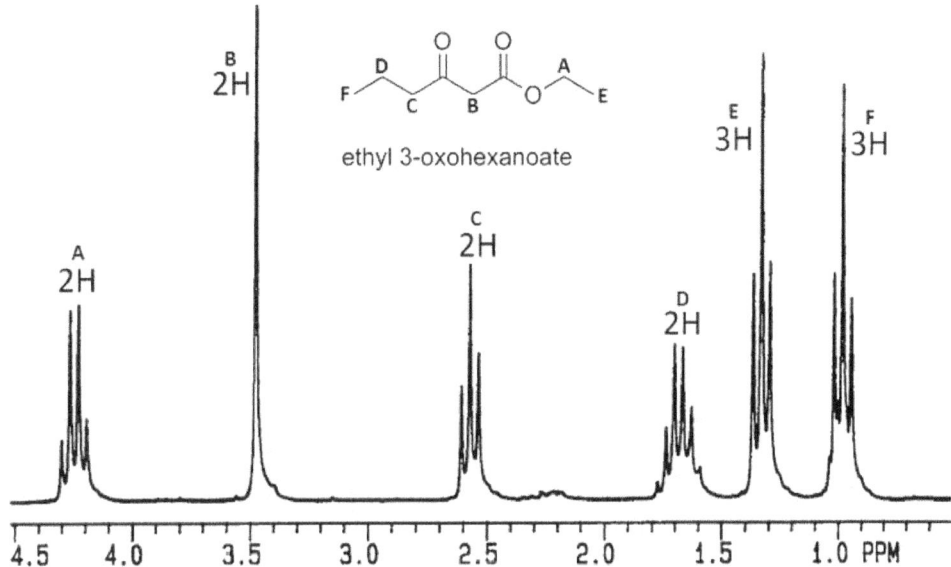

Que 33: For the following compound indicates the number of signals that would appear in its proton NMR spectrum.

ethyl propanoate

Ans: there are four types of protons and numbers of signals are:2H quartet, 2H quartet, two 3H triplet,

51

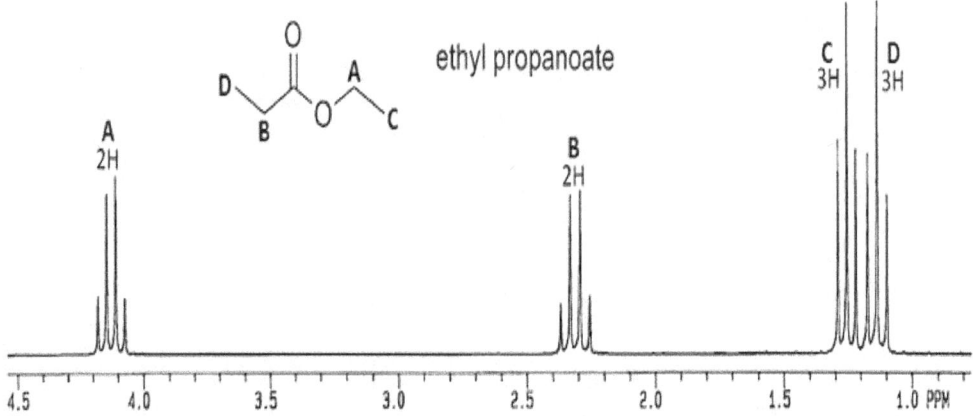

Que 34: For the methyl propanoate indicates the number of signals that would appear in its proton NMR spectrum

Ans: There are three types of protons as indicated and numbers of signals are: 3H singlet, 2H quartet, 3H triplet

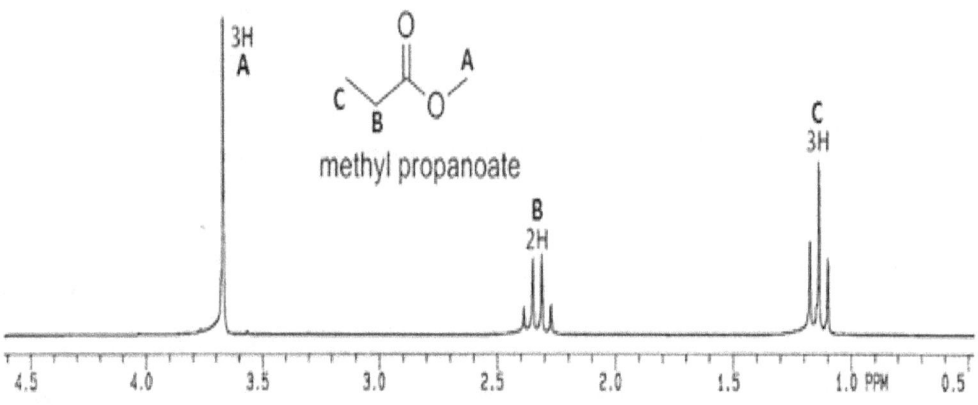

Que 35: For the 4-methyl-2-pentanol indicates the number of signals that would appear in its proton NMR spectrum

52

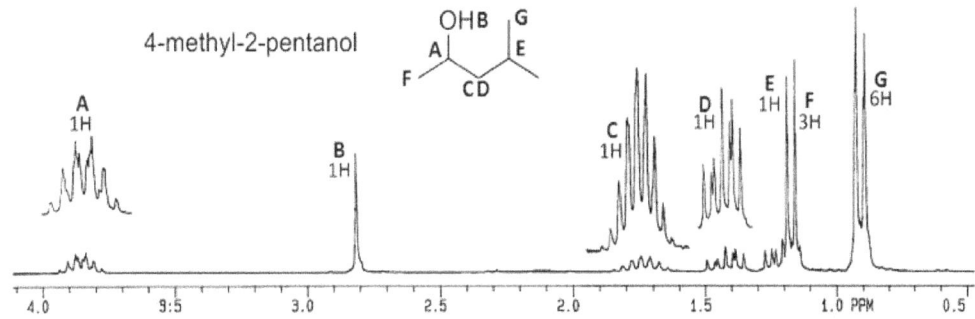

4-methyl-2-pentanol

Que 36: For the following compound indicates the number of signals that would appear in its proton NMR spectrum.

$$CH_3CH_2CH_2CH_2Cl$$

Ans: There are four types of protons and numbers of signals are : 2H triplet, 2H, pentet, 2H sextet, 3H triplet

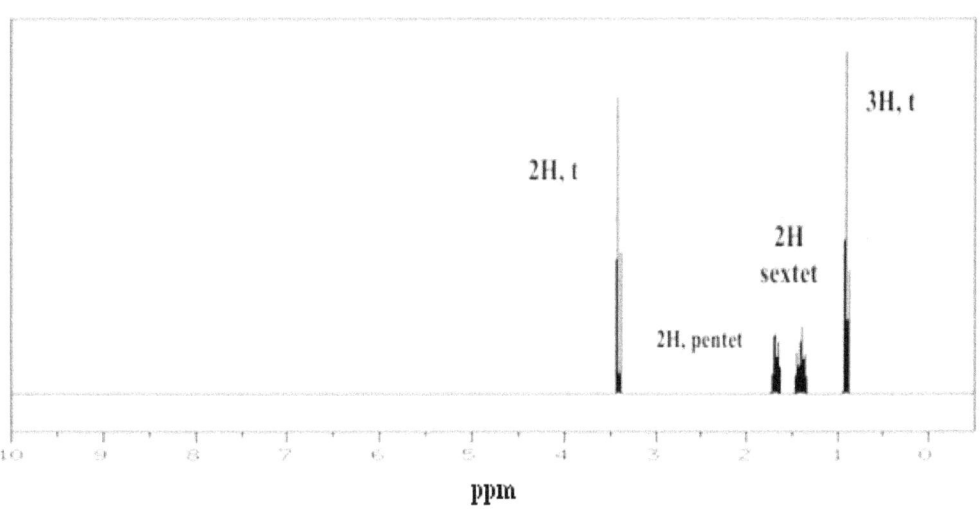

ppm

Que 37: For the following compound indicates the number of signals that would appear in its proton NMR spectrum

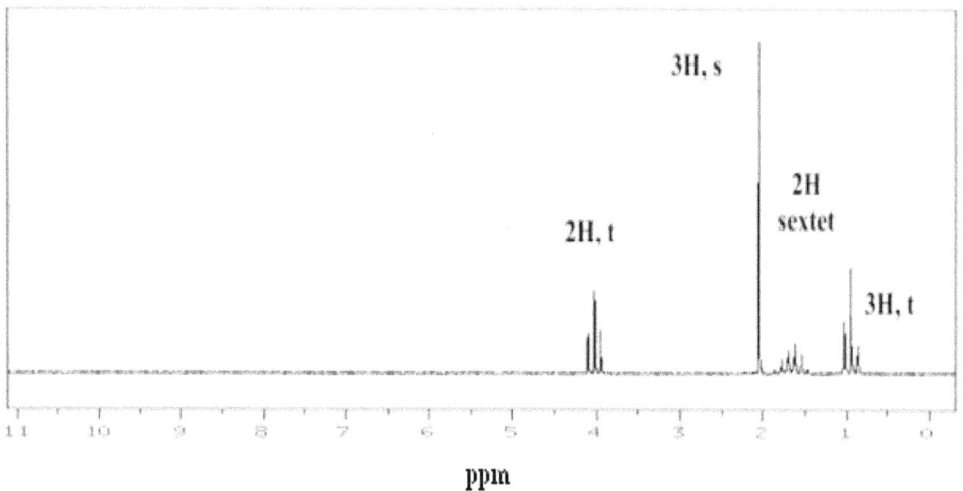

Ans: There are four types of protons and numbers of signals are :3H singlet, 2H triplet, 2H sextet, 3H triplet

Que 38: For the following compound indicates the number of signals that would appear in its proton NMR spectrum.

Ans There are three types of protons and numbers of signals are 3H singlet, 1h multiplet, and 6H doublet

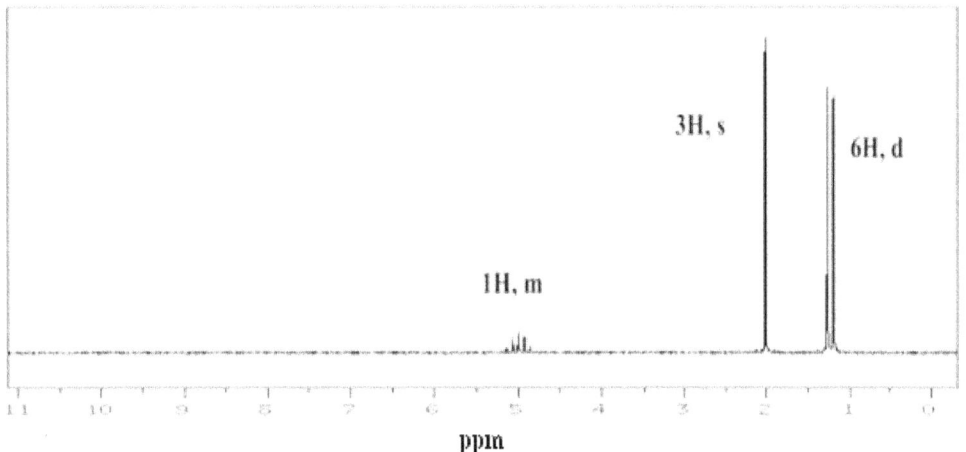

Que 39: For the following compound indicates the number of signals that would appear in its proton NMR spectrum.

$$H_3C-\overset{\displaystyle Cl}{\underset{\displaystyle H}{C}}-CH_2-CH_3$$

Ans: There are four types of protons and numbers of signals are: 3H doublet, 1H multiplet, 2H pentet, and 3H triplet as indicated in given figure

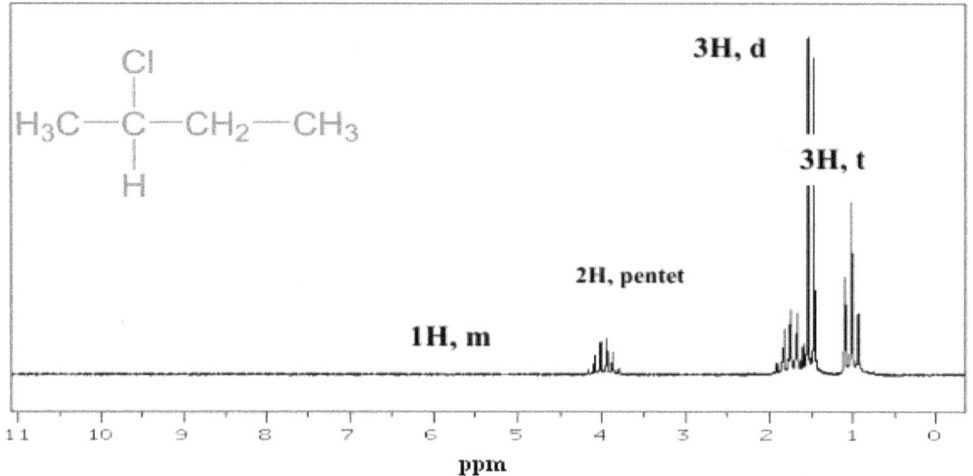

Que 40: For the following compound indicates the number of signals that would appear in its proton NMR spectrum.

$$\begin{array}{c} CH_3 \\ | \\ H-C-CH_3 \\ | \\ \bigcirc \end{array}$$

Ans: There are three types of protons and numbers of signals are: 1H multiplet, 6H doublet, 5H multiplet

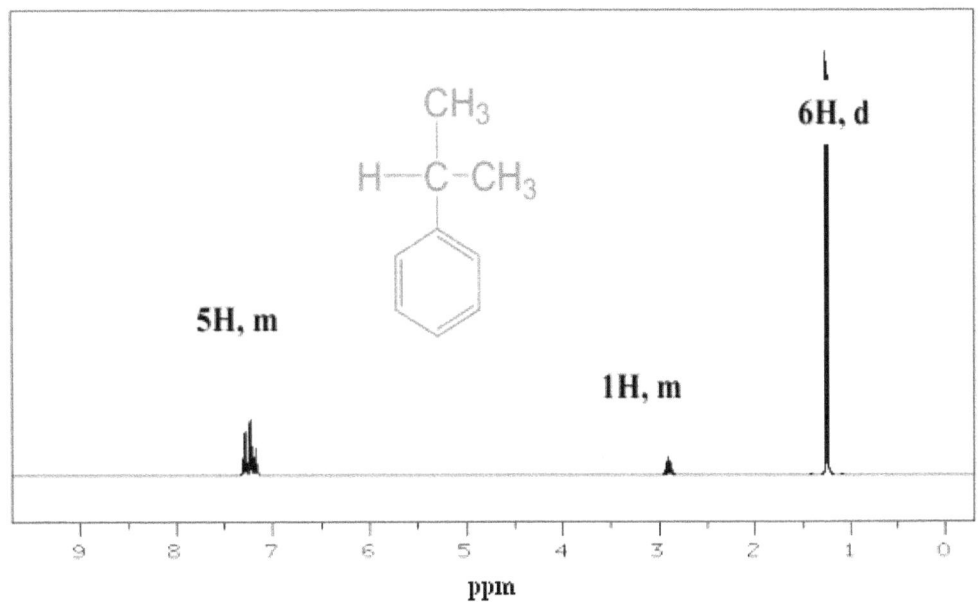

Que 41: For the following compound indicates the number of signals that would appear in its proton NMR spectrum

Ans: there are five types of protons as indicated in figure and numbers of signals are : 5H multiplet, 1H sextet, 2H doublet, 3H doublet, 1H singlet

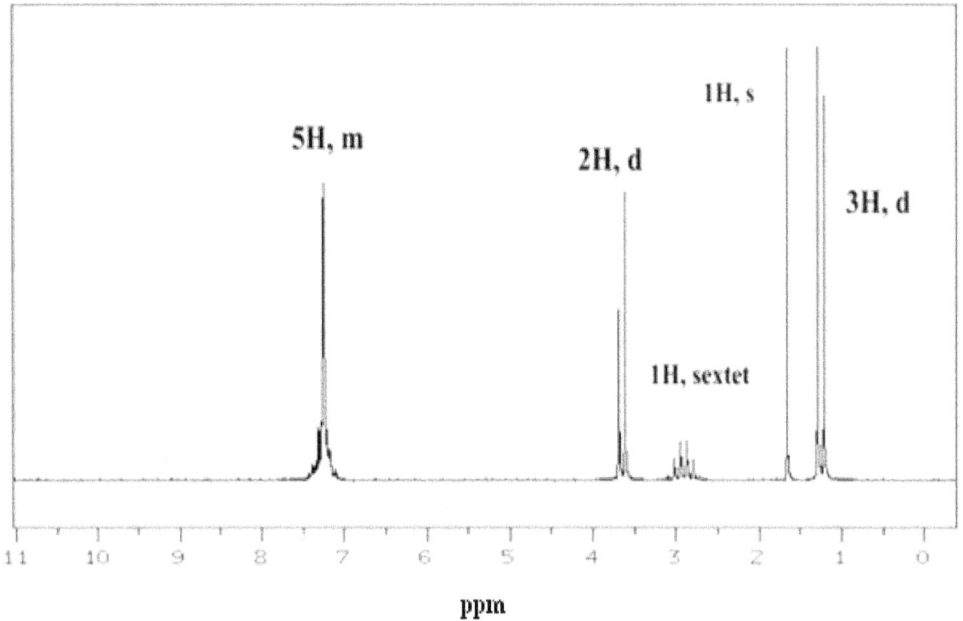

Que 42: For the following compound indicates the number of signals that would appear in its proton NMR spectrum.

Ans: there are five types of protons and signals are: 6H doublet, 1H septet, 2H triplet, 2H sextet, 3H triplet

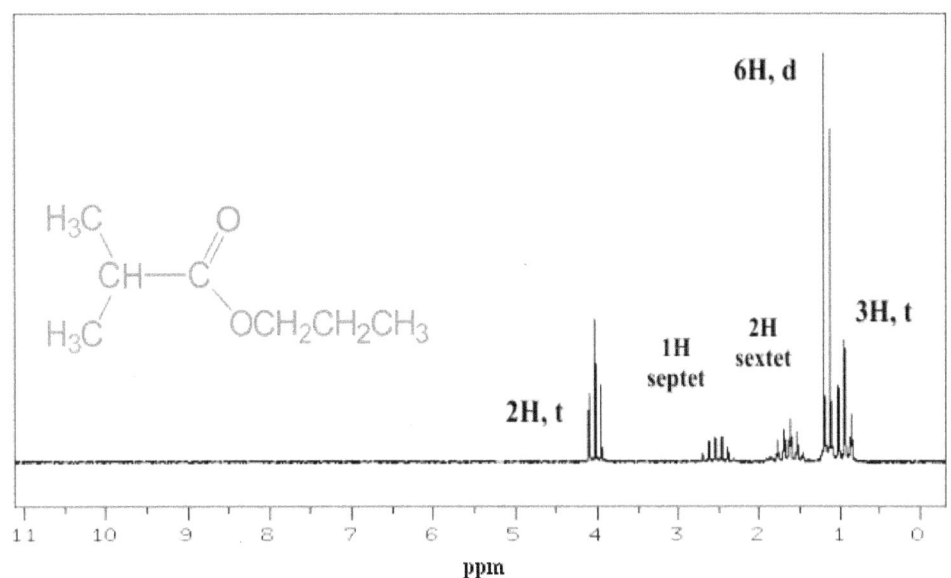

Que 43: For the 2-methyl-1-propanol indicates the number of signals that would appear in its proton NMR spectrum

Ans: There are four types of protons as indicated and numbers of

signals are: 1H singlet, 2H doublet, 1H multiplet, and 6h doublet

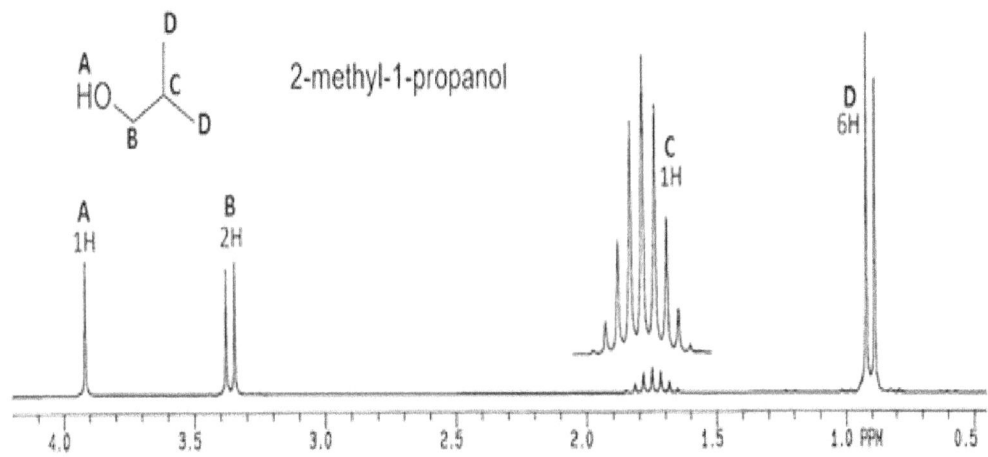

Que 44: For the 4-butyoxybenzaldehyde indicates the number of signals that would appear in its proton NMR spectrum.

Ans: There seven types of protons as indicated and numbers of signals

are : 1H singlet, 2H doublet, 2H doublet,2H triplet, 2H pentet, 2H

sextet, and 3H triplet,

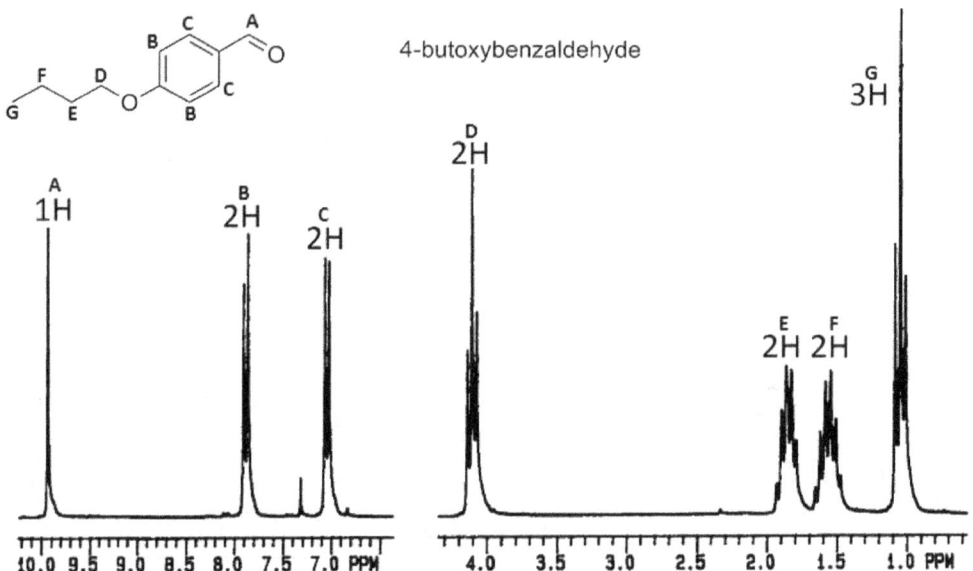

4-butoxybenzaldehyde

Que 45:For the following compound indicate the number of signals that would appear in its proton NMR spectrum.

6-methyl-5-heptane-2-one

Ans: There are five types of protons as indicated and signals

are:Three 3H singlet, 1H triplet, 2H quartet, and 2H triplet

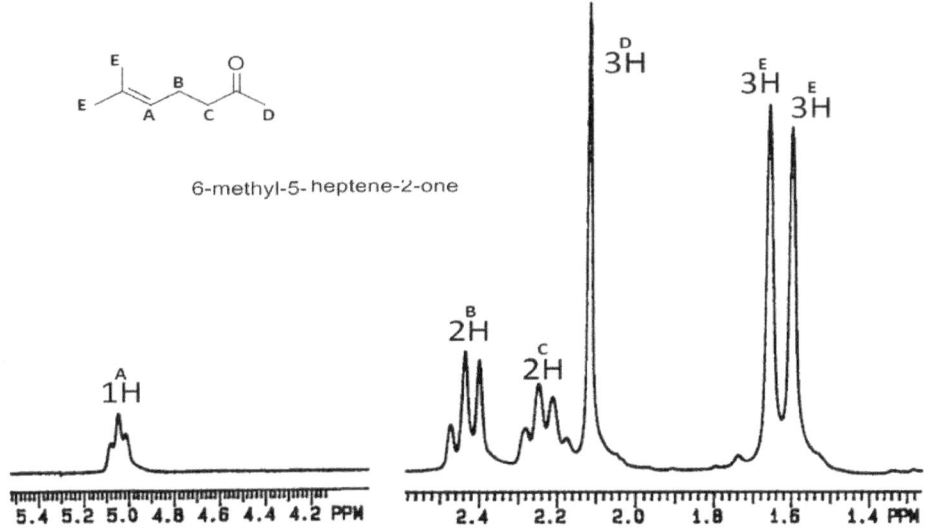

6-methyl-5-heptene-2-one

Que 46:For the 2- heptanone indicate the number of signals that would appear in its proton NMR spectrum.

Ans: there are six types of proton in 2-heptanone as indicated and signals are:3H singlet, 2H triplet, two 2H pentet, 2H sextet, and 3H triplet

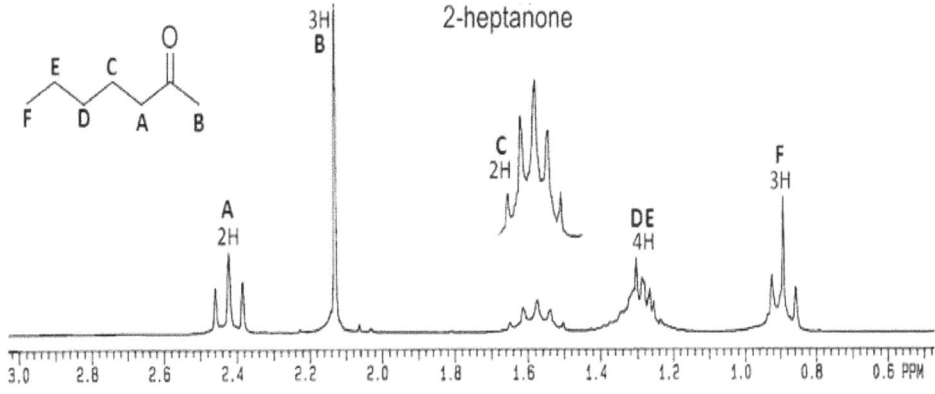

Que 47: For the 2- pentanone indicate the number of signals that would appear in its proton NMR spectrum.

Ans: there are four types of protons as indicated and signals are: 3H singlet, 2H triplet, 2H sextet, and 3H triplet

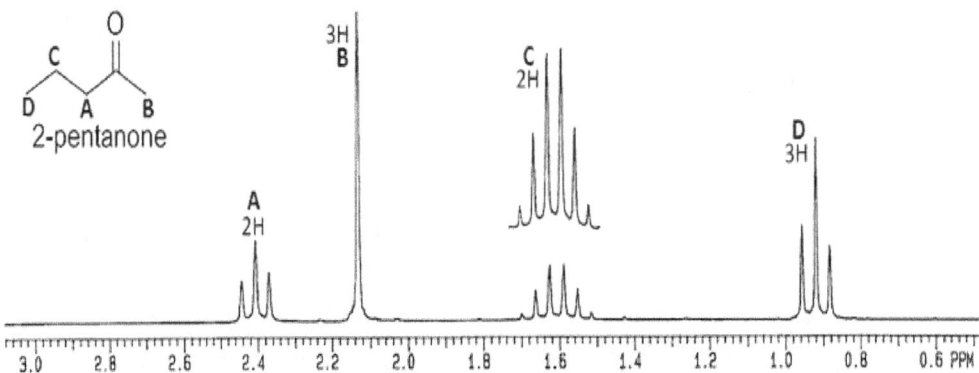

Que 48: For the following compound indicates the number of signals that would appear in its proton NMR spectrum

Ans: 6H doublet, 1H septet, 2H doublet,6H Doublet, 1H septet,

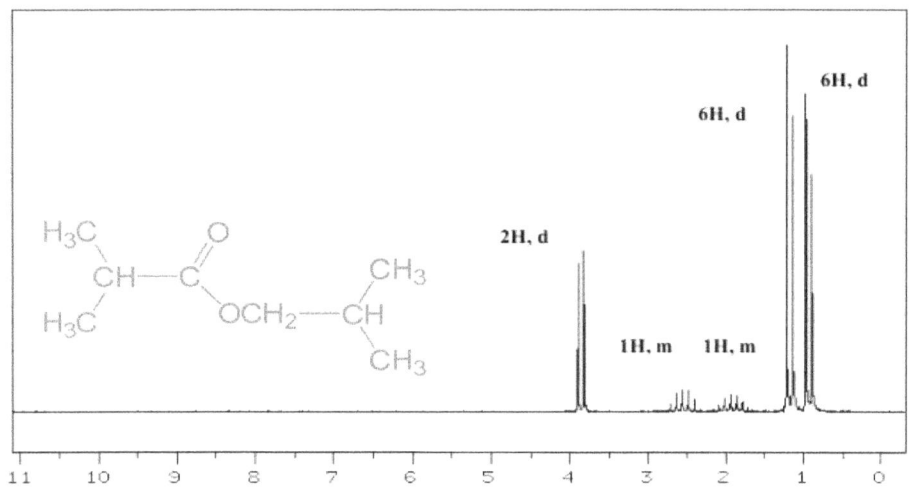

Que 49: For the following compound indicates the number of signals that would appear in its proton NMR spectrum
Ans:

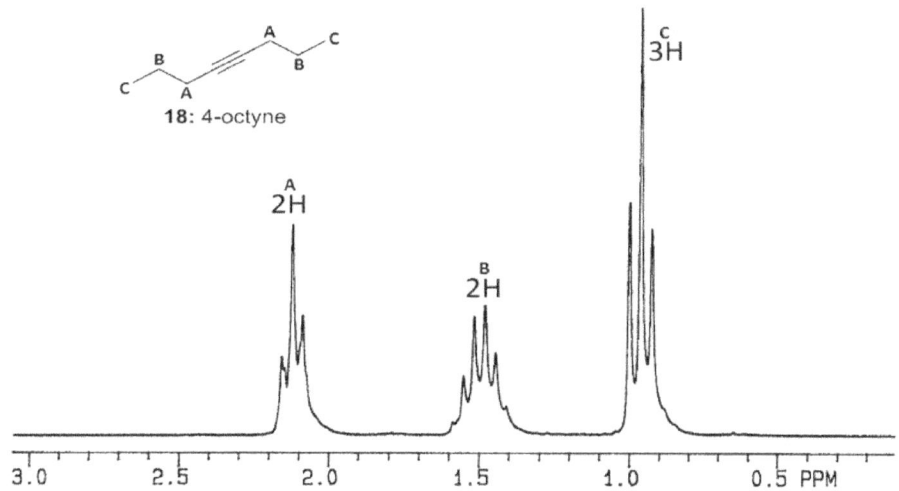

18: 4-octyne

Que 50: For the following compound indicates the number of signals that would appear in its proton NMR spectrum.

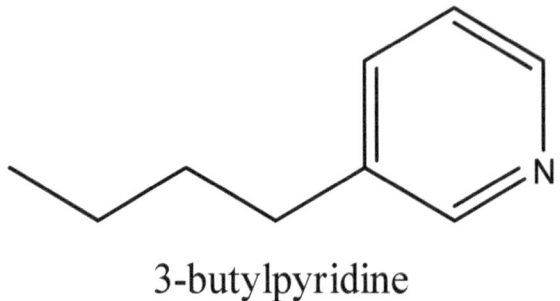

3-butylpyridine

Ans:

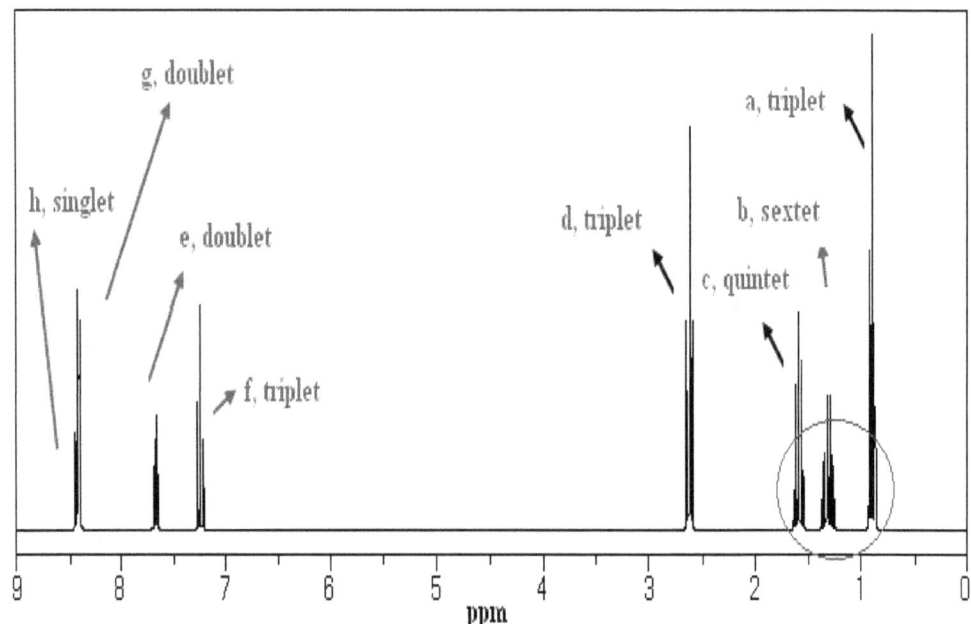

Que 51: For the following compound indicates the number of signals that would appear in its proton NMR spectrum.

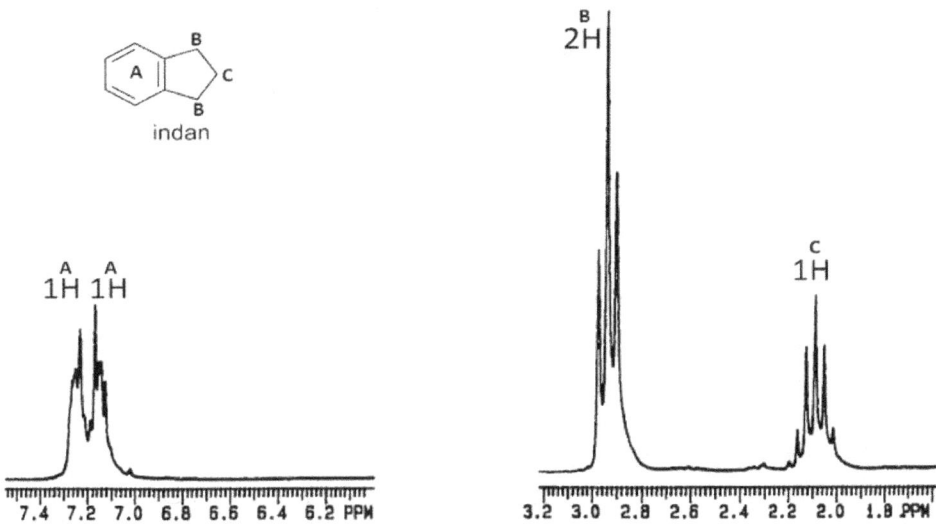

indan

Que 52: For the following compound indicates the number of signals that would appear in its proton NMR spectrum.

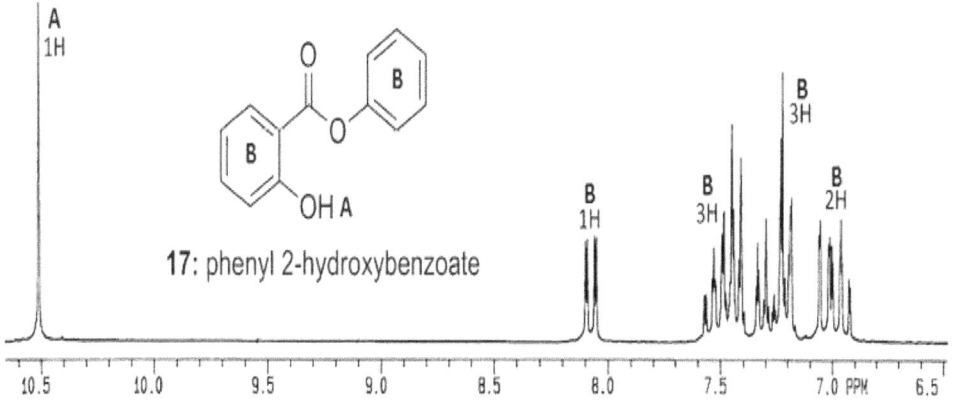

17: phenyl 2-hydroxybenzoate

Que 53: For the following compound indicates the number of signals that would appear in its proton NMR spectrum.

$$CH_3CH_2-\bigcirc-\overset{\overset{\displaystyle O}{\parallel}}{C}-OH$$

^{1}H NMR:

1-2 ppm, area 3H, triplet (methyl)

2-3 ppm, area 2H, quartet (methylene)

7-8 ppm, area 4,H multiplet (aromatic)

11-12 ppm, area 1H, singlet (carboxylic acid)

Que 54: For the following compound indicates the number of signals that would appear in its proton NMR spectrum.

$$CH_3-O\overset{\overset{\displaystyle CH_3}{|}}{\underset{}{C}}\overset{\overset{\displaystyle O}{\parallel}}{C}-H$$

^{1}H NMR:

1-2 ppm, area 3H, doublet (methyl)

2-3 ppm, area 2H, triplet (methylene) (actually a doublet of doublets)

3-4 ppm, area 3H, singlet (methoxy)

3-4 ppm, area 1H, multiplet (methine - CH) (actually a triplet of

quartets)

9-10 ppm, area 1H, triplet (aldehyde)

Que 55: For the following compound indicates the number of signals that would appear in its proton NMR spectrum.

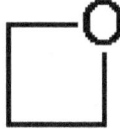

^{1}H NMR:

2.72 ppm, area 2H, quintet

4.73 ppm, area 4H, triplet

Que 56: **For the following compound indicates the number of signals that would appear in its proton NMR spectrum.**

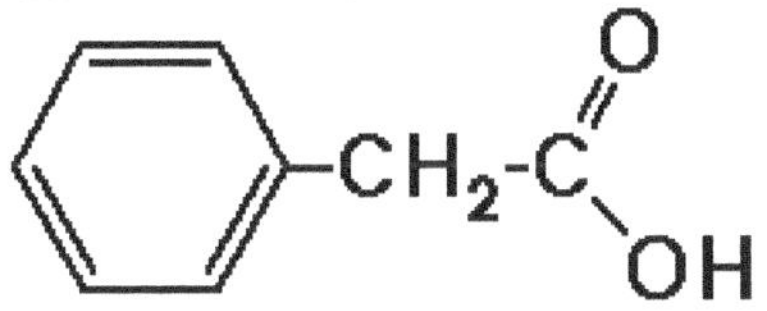

^{1}H NMR:

11.0 ppm, area 1H, singlet

7.0 ppm, area 5H, multiplet

3.0 ppm, area 2H, singlet

Que 57: **For the following compound indicates the number of signals that would appear in its proton NMR spectrum.**

^{1}H NMR:
7.05 ppm, area 4H, singlet
2.45 ppm, area 4H, quartet
1.05 ppm, area 6H, triplet

Que 58: **For the following compound indicates the number of signals that would appear in its proton NMR spectrum.**

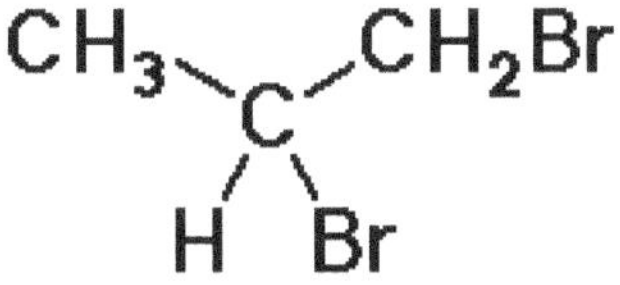

^{1}H NMR:

3.80 ppm, area 1H, multiplet

3.50 ppm, area 2H, doublet

1.12 ppm, area 3H, doublet

Que 59: For the following compound indicates the number of signals that would appear in its proton NMR spectrum.

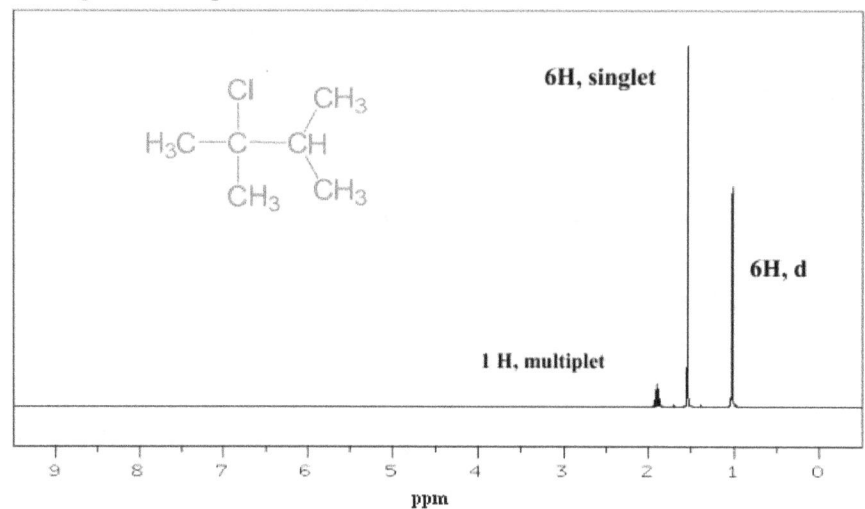

^{1}H NMR:

4.92 ppm, area 1H, singlet,   5.11 ppm, area 1H, singlet,

1.33 ppm, area 2H, triplet   1.96, area 2H, triplet

Que 60: For the following compound indicates the number of signals that would appear in its proton NMR spectrum

6H singlet, 1H septet, 6H doublet

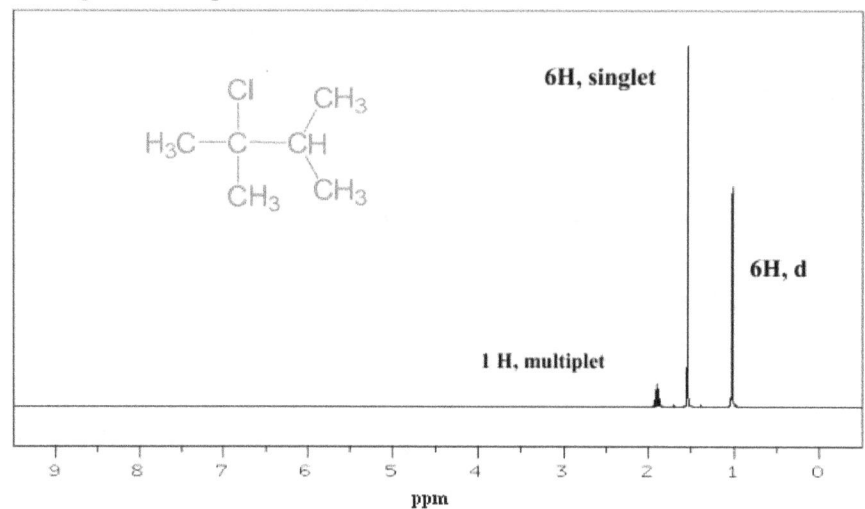

Que 61: **For the following compound indicates the number of signals that would appear in its proton NMR spectrum.**

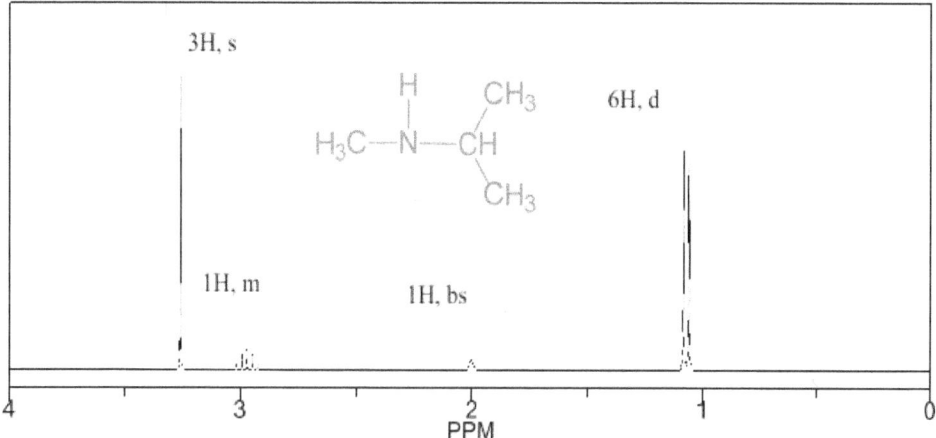

Isopropyl methylamine

Que 62: For the following compound indicates the number of signals that would appear in its proton NMR spectrum.

$$CH_3CH_2\text{-}Br$$

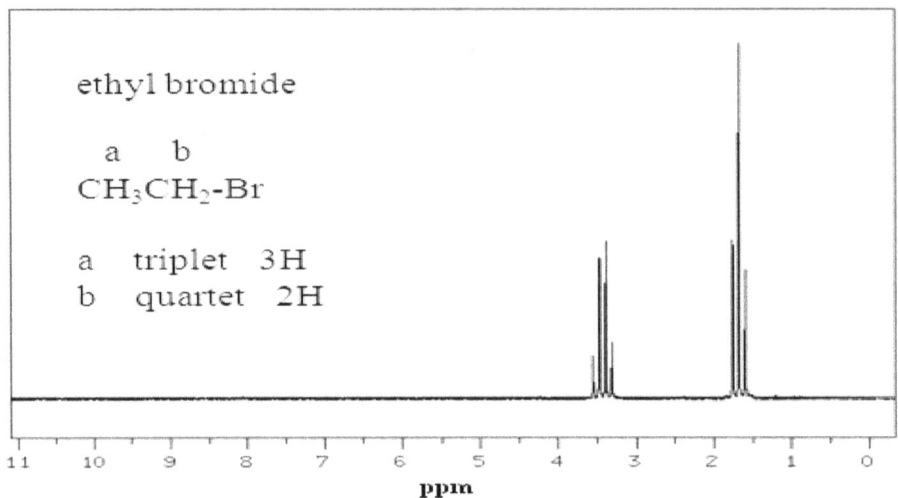

Que 63: **For the following compound indicates the number of signals that would appear in its proton NMR spectrum.**

$CH_3CH_2CH_2$-Br

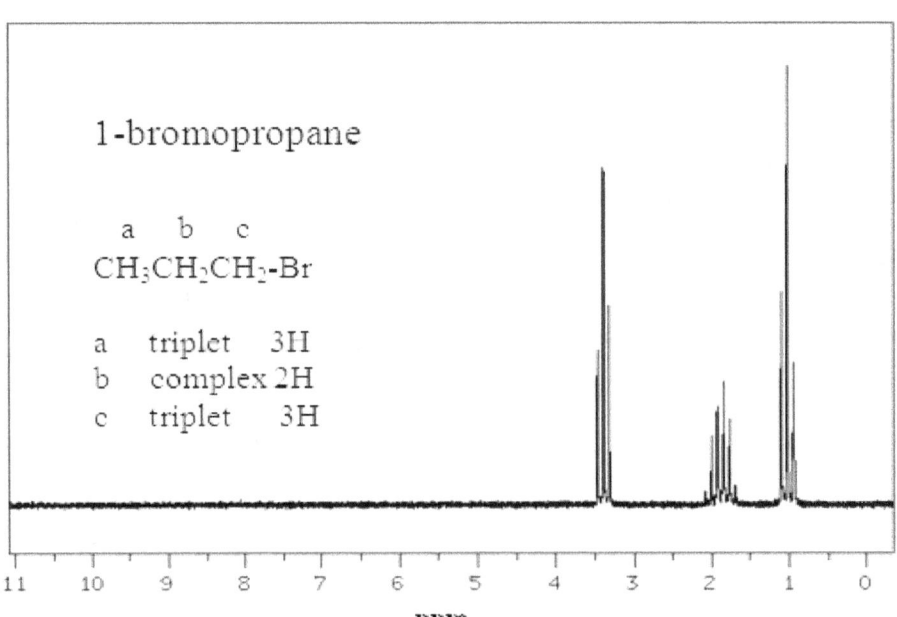

Que 64: **For the following compound indicates the number of signals that would appear in its proton NMR spectrum**

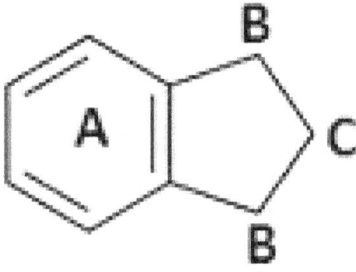

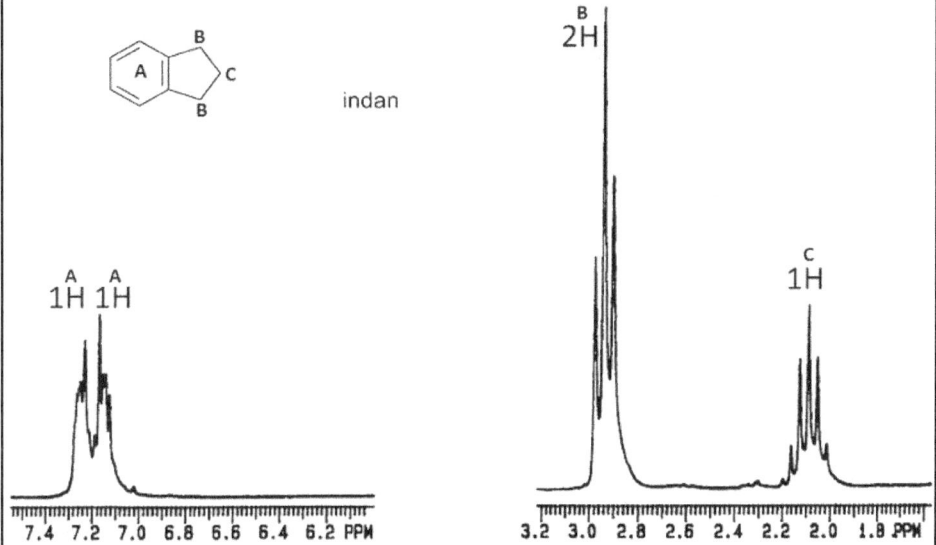

Que 65: For the following compound indicates the number of signals that would appear in its proton NMR spectrum

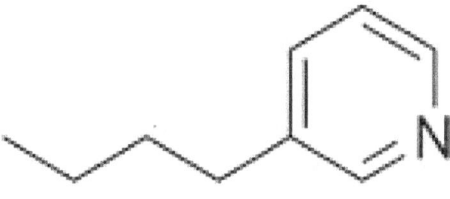

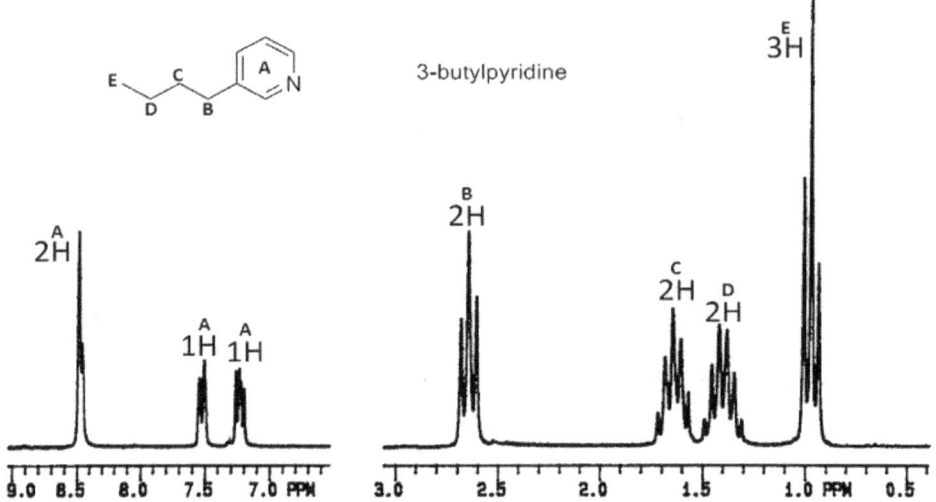

3-butylpyridine

Que 66: For the following compound indicates the number of signals that would appear in its proton NMR spectrum.

$$CH_3CHCH_3$$
$$Cl$$

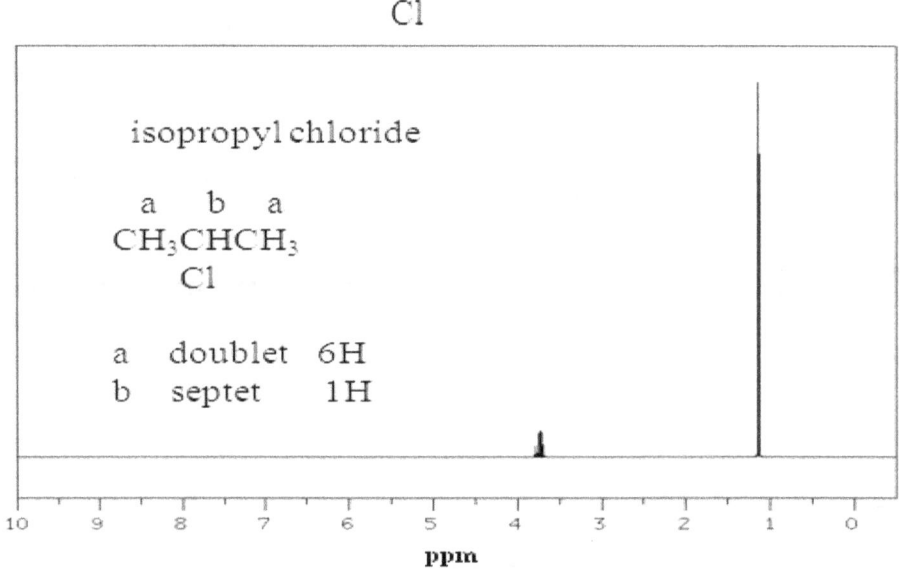

isopropyl chloride

a   b   a
$$CH_3CHCH_3$$
$$Cl$$

a   doublet   6H
b   septet   1H

Que 67: For the following compound indicates the number of signals that would appear in its proton NMR spectrum.

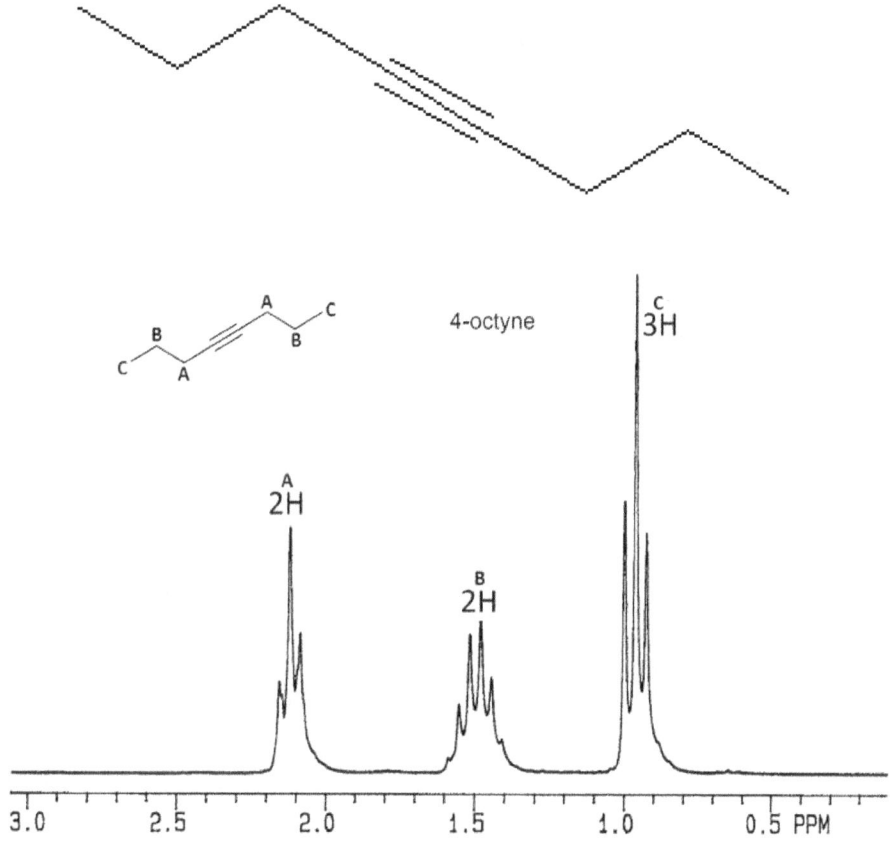

4-octyne

Que 68: For the following compound indicates the number of signals that would appear in its proton NMR spectrum.

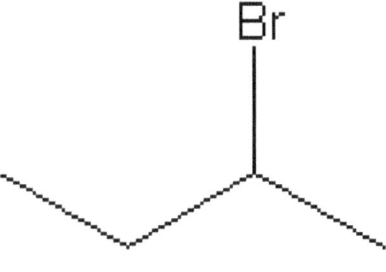

73

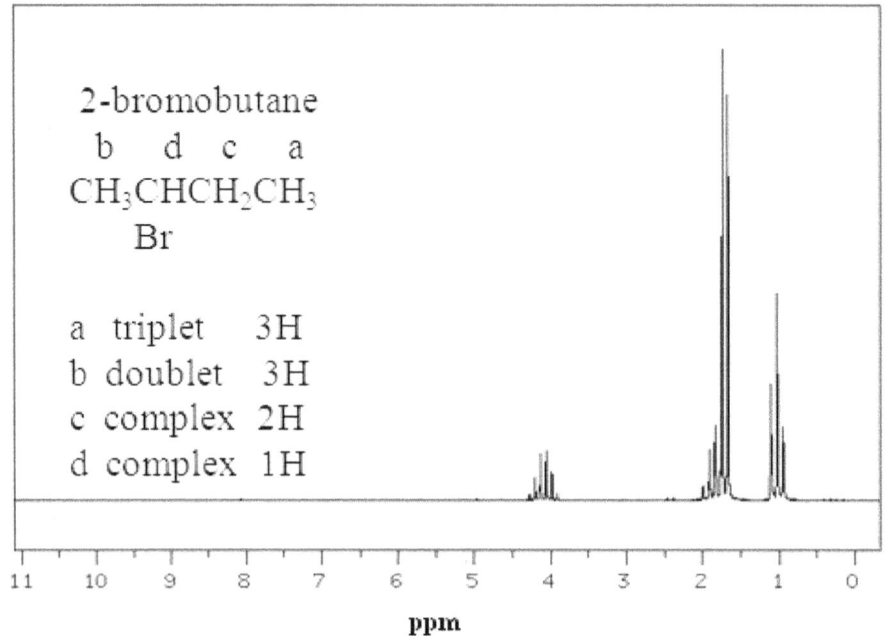

2-bromobutane

b   d   c   a
CH₃CHCH₂CH₃
   Br

a triplet   3H
b doublet 3H
c complex 2H
d complex 1H

ppm

Que 69: For the following compound indicates the number of signals that would appear in its proton NMR spectrum.

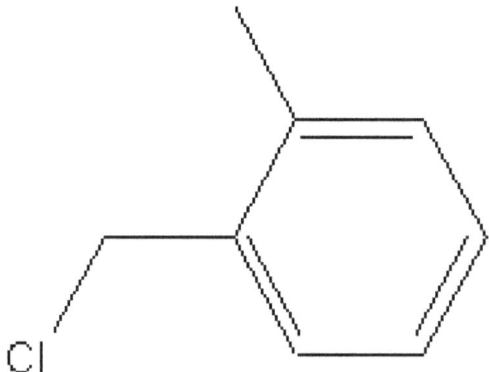

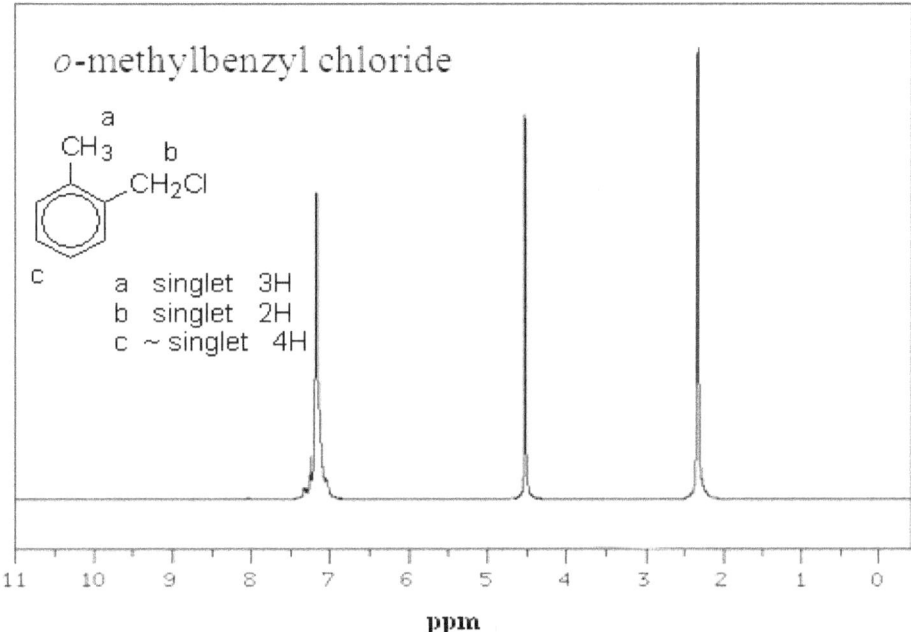

o-methylbenzyl chloride

a   singlet   3H
b   singlet   2H
c ~ singlet   4H

ppm

Que 70: For the following compound indicates the number of signals that would appear in its proton NMR spectrum.

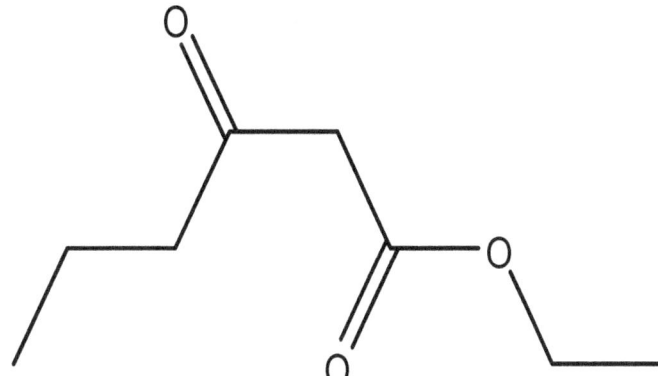

75

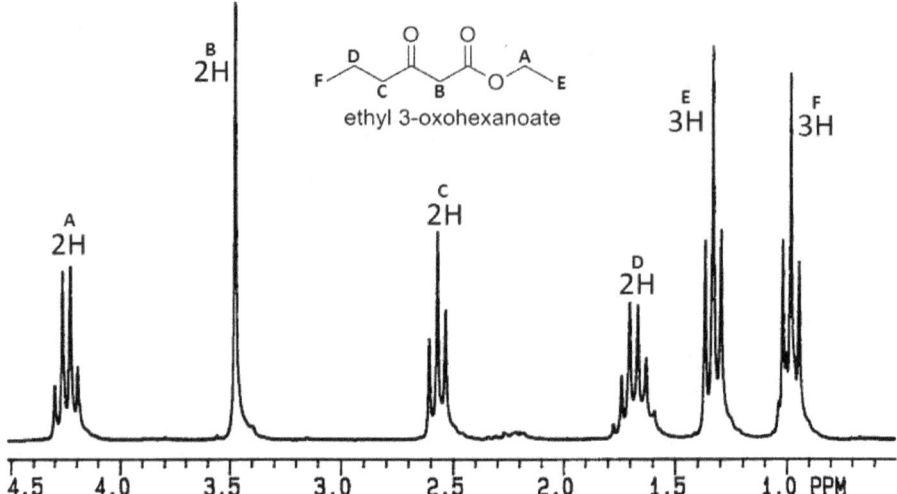

ethyl 3-oxohexanoate

Que 71: For the following compound indicates the number of signals that would appear in its proton NMR spectrum.

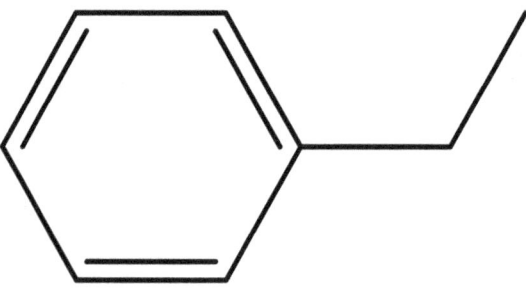

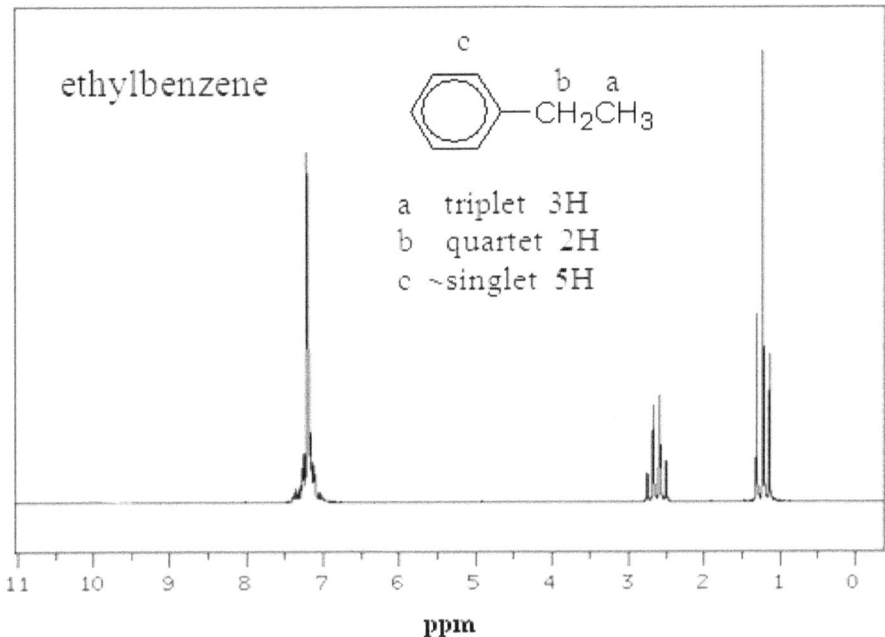

ethylbenzene

a   triplet 3H
b   quartet 2H
c   ~singlet 5H

ppm

Que 72: For the following compound indicates the number of signals that would appear in its proton NMR spectrum.

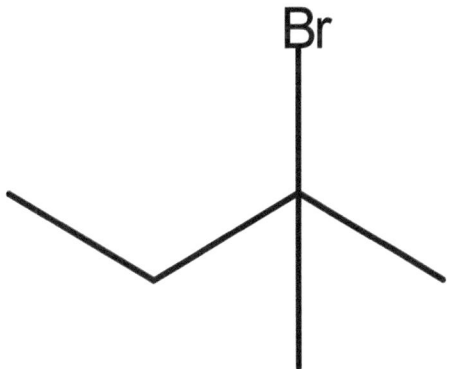

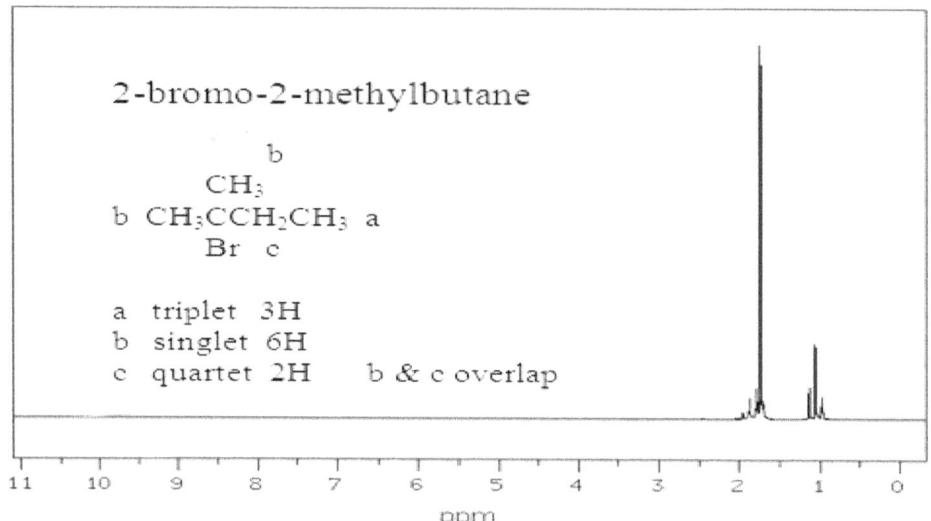

2-bromo-2-methylbutane

b
CH₃
b CH₃CCH₂CH₃ a
Br c

a triplet 3H
b singlet 6H
c quartet 2H   b & c overlap

Que 73: For the following compound indicates the number of signals that would appear in its proton NMR spectrum.

CH₃CH₂CH₂-O-CH₂CH₂CH₃

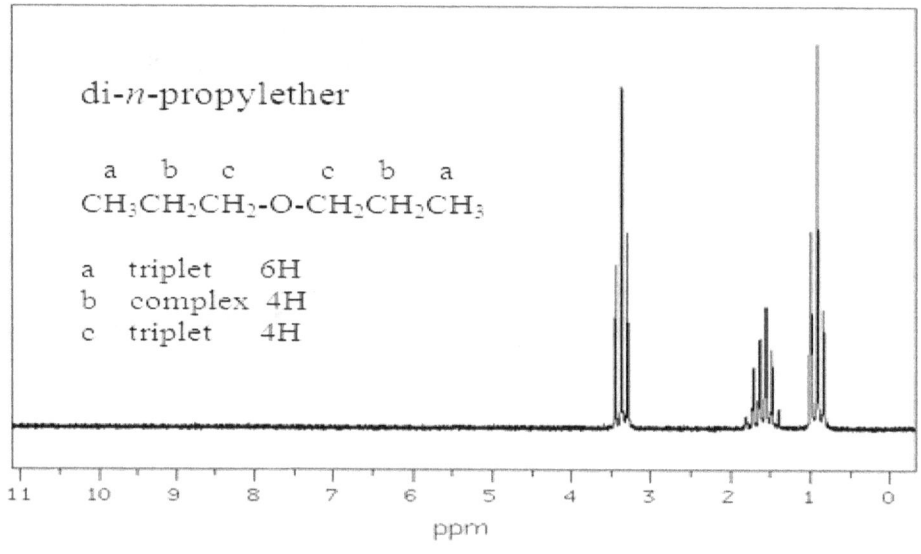

di-*n*-propylether

a   b   c   c   b   a
CH₃CH₂CH₂-O-CH₂CH₂CH₃

a   triplet   6H
b   complex 4H
c   triplet   4H

Que 74: For the following compound indicates the number of signals that would appear in its proton NMR spectrum.

CH₃CH₂CH₂-OH

78

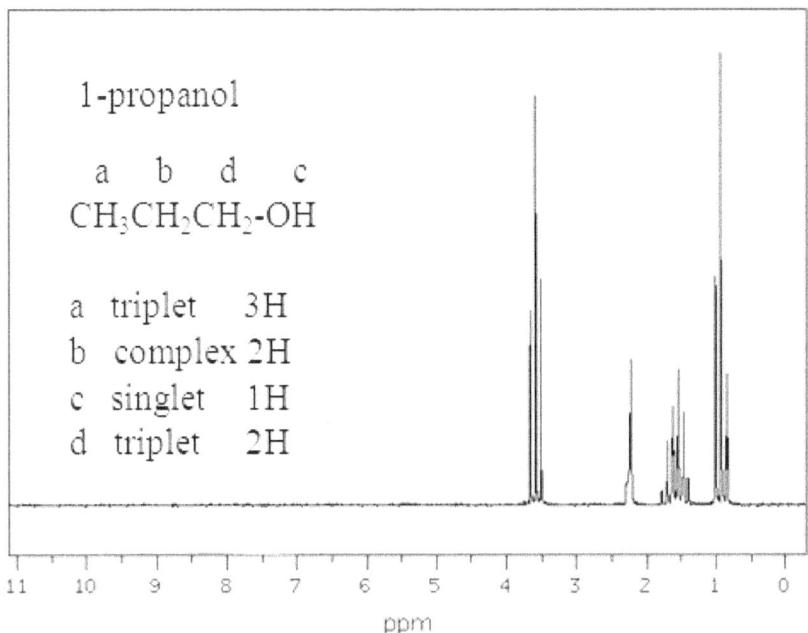

1-propanol

a   b   d   c
$CH_3CH_2CH_2$-OH

a   triplet   3H
b   complex 2H
c   singlet   1H
d   triplet   2H

Que 75: For the following compound indicates the number of signals that would appear in its proton NMR spectrum.

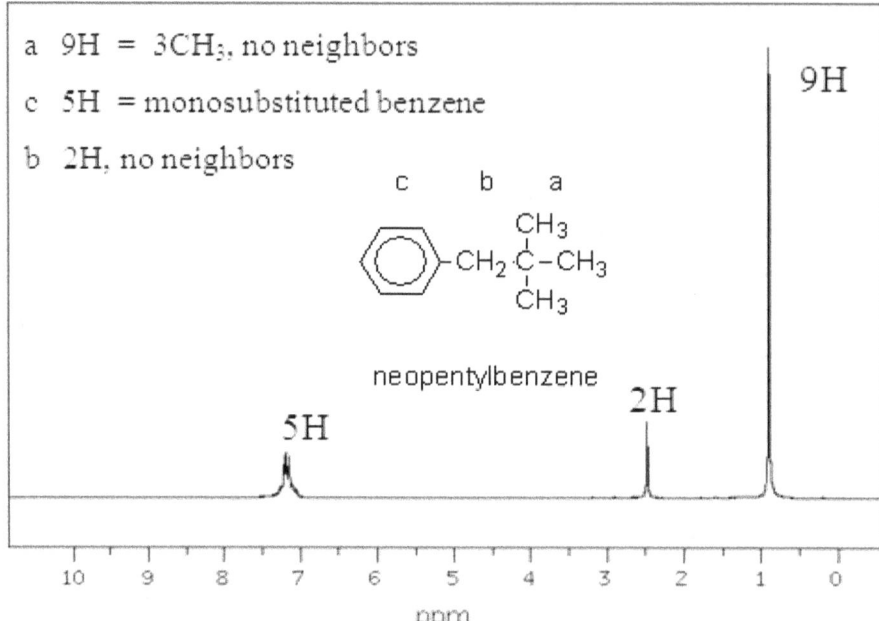

a 9H = 3CH₃, no neighbors

c 5H = monosubstituted benzene

b 2H, no neighbors

neopentylbenzene

Que 76: For the following compound indicates the number of signals that would appear in its proton NMR spectrum.

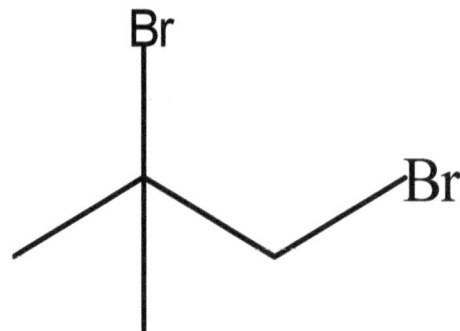

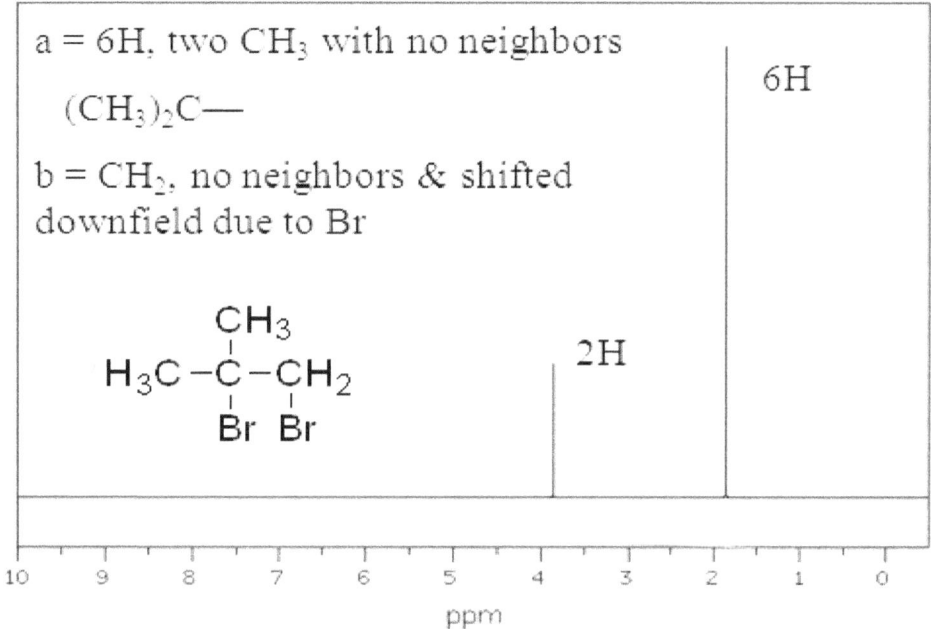

a = 6H, two CH$_3$ with no neighbors

(CH$_3$)$_2$C—

b = CH$_2$, no neighbors & shifted downfield due to Br

Que 77: For the following compound indicates the number of signals that would appear in its proton NMR spectrum.

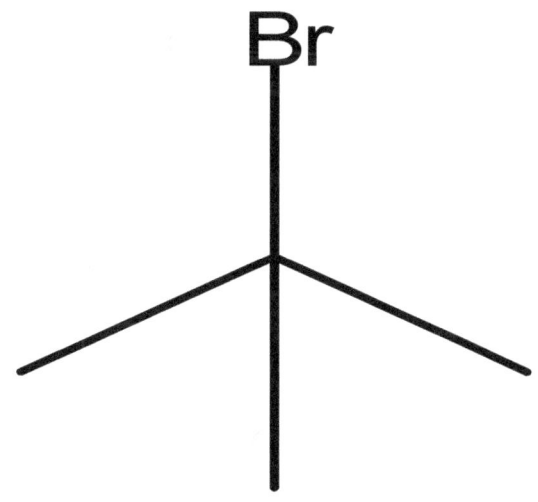

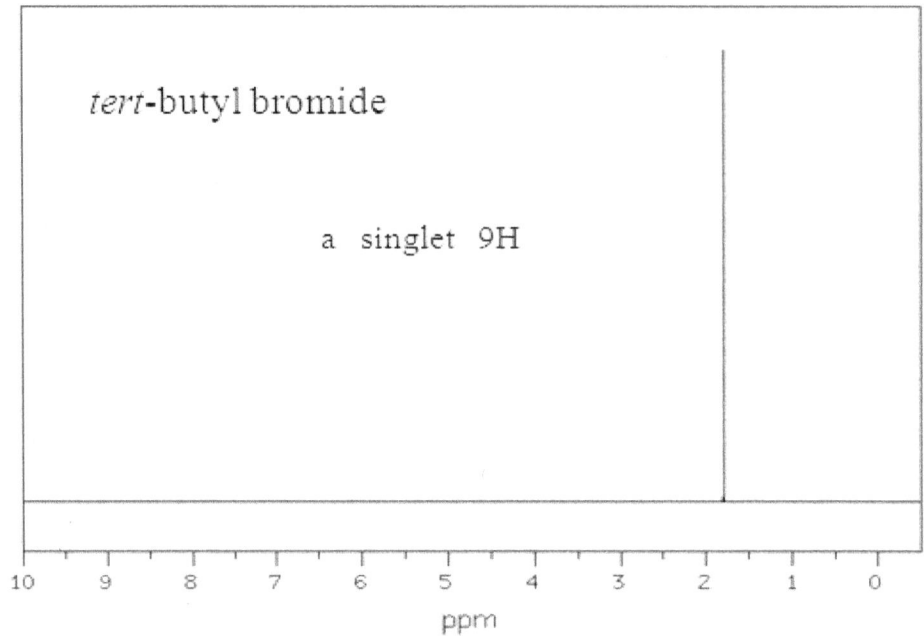

tert-butyl bromide

a singlet 9H

Que 78: For the following compound indicates the number of signals that would appear in its proton NMR spectrum.

H_3C—⬡—CH_3

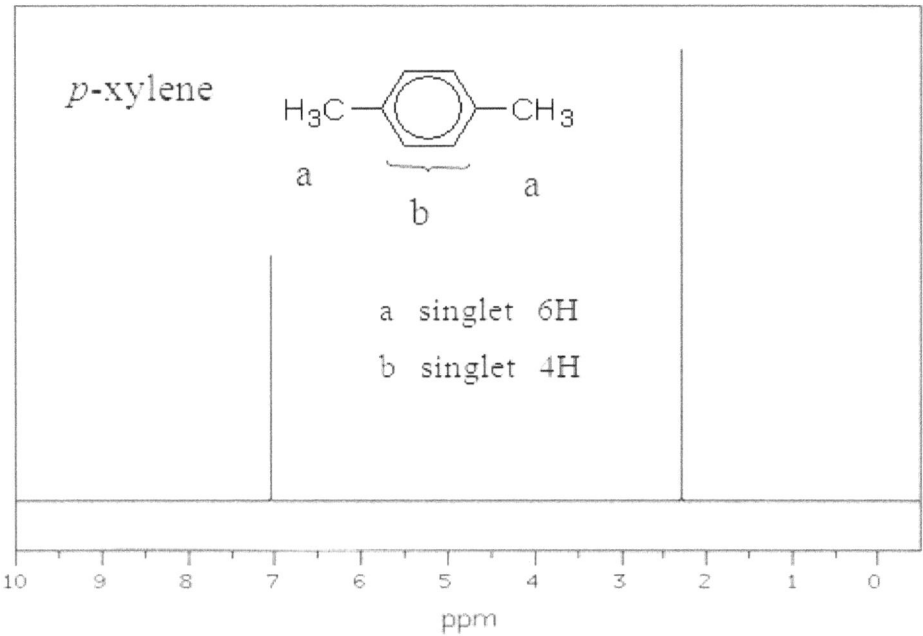

p-xylene

a singlet 6H

b singlet 4H

Que 79: For the following compound indicates the number of signals that would appear in its proton NMR spectrum.

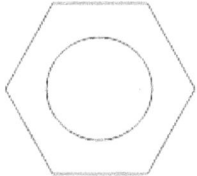

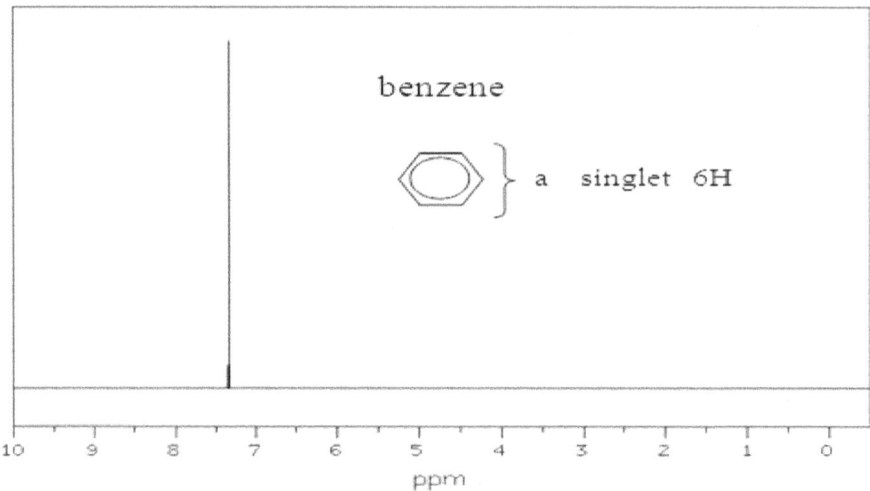

Que 80: For the following compound indicates the number of signals that would appear in its proton NMR spectrum.

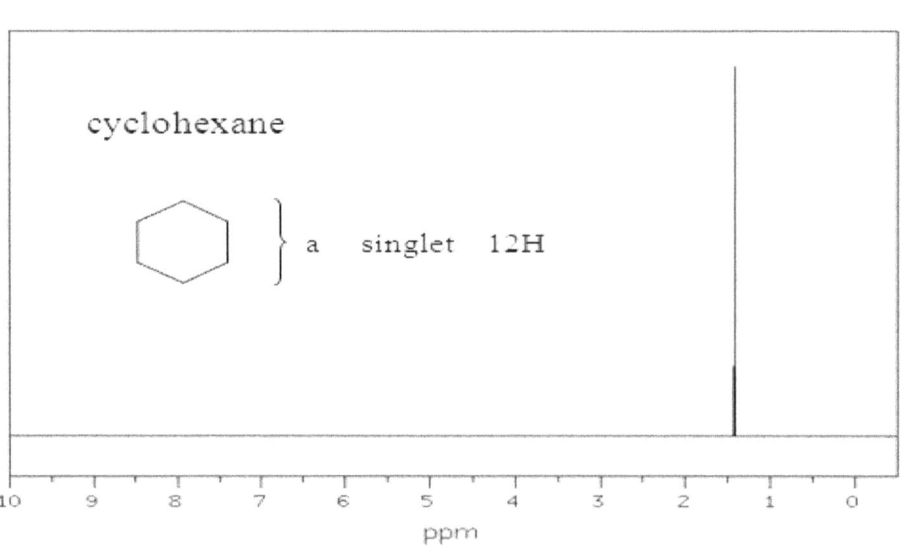

Que 81: For the following compound indicates the number of signals that would appear in its proton NMR spectrum.

84

CH_3CH_2-Br

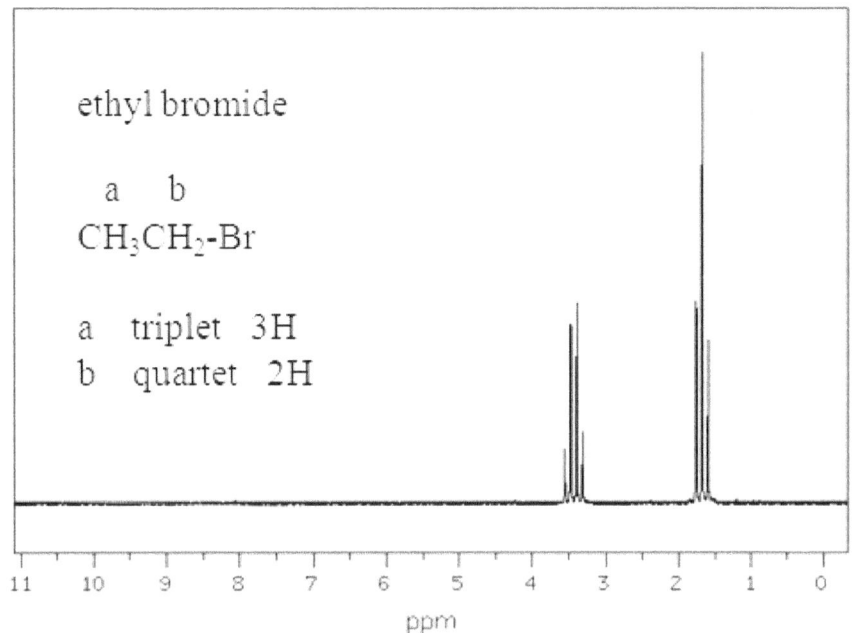

ethyl bromide

  a   b

CH_3CH_2-Br

a triplet 3H
b quartet 2H

Que 82: For the following compound indicates the number of signals that would appear in its proton NMR spectrum.

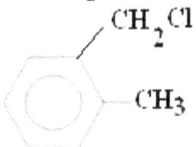

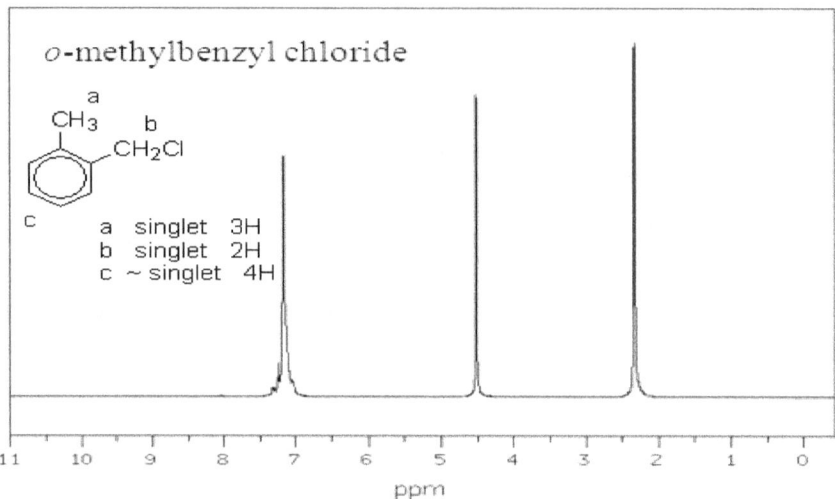

o-methylbenzyl chloride

a singlet 3H
b singlet 2H
c ~ singlet 4H

Que 83: For the following compound indicates the number of signals that would appear in its proton NMR spectrum.

CH_2OH

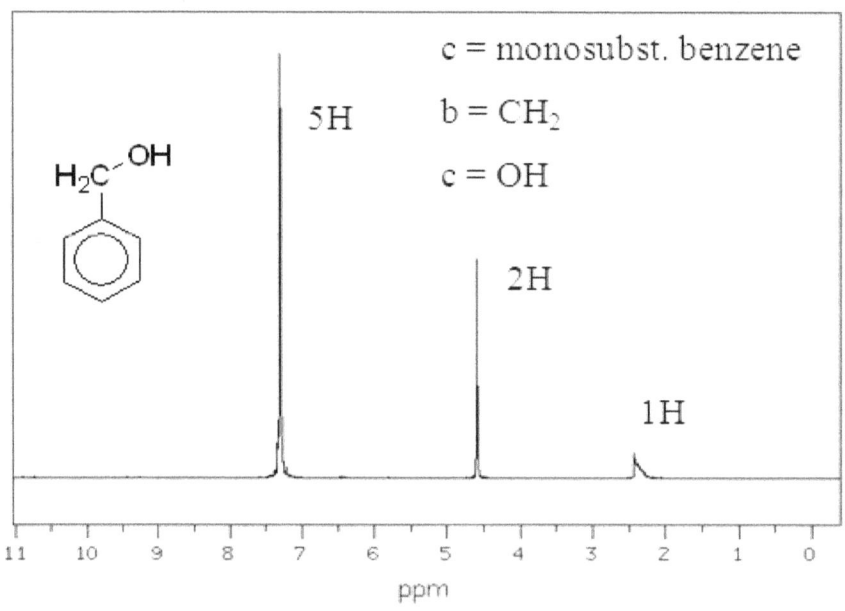

c = monosubst. benzene

b = CH_2

c = OH

5H

2H

1H

86

Que 84: For the following compound indicates the number of signals that would appear in its proton NMR spectrum.

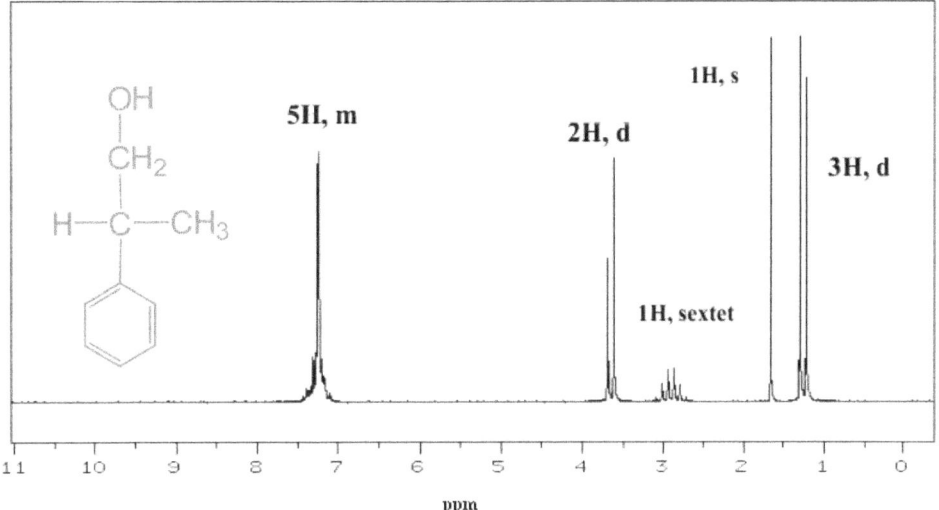

Que 85: For the following compound indicates the number of signals that would appear in its proton NMR spectrum.

$$CH_3 CHCl_2$$

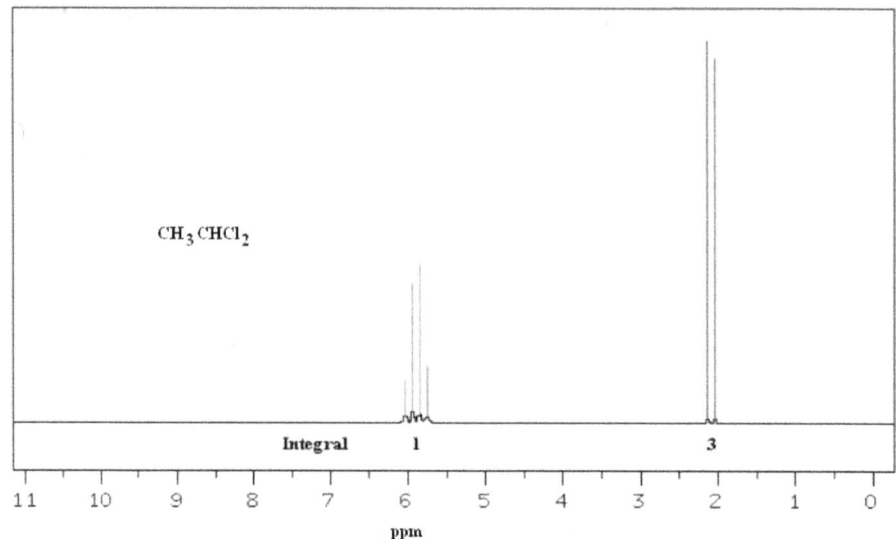

^{1}H NMR of Benzene

In benzene, the protons on the aromatic ring are shifted downfield. For example, the six protons in benzene are magnetically and chemically equivalent and appear at 7.33 ppm. This is farther downfield than alkene protons, which appear between 4.5-6.5 ppm.

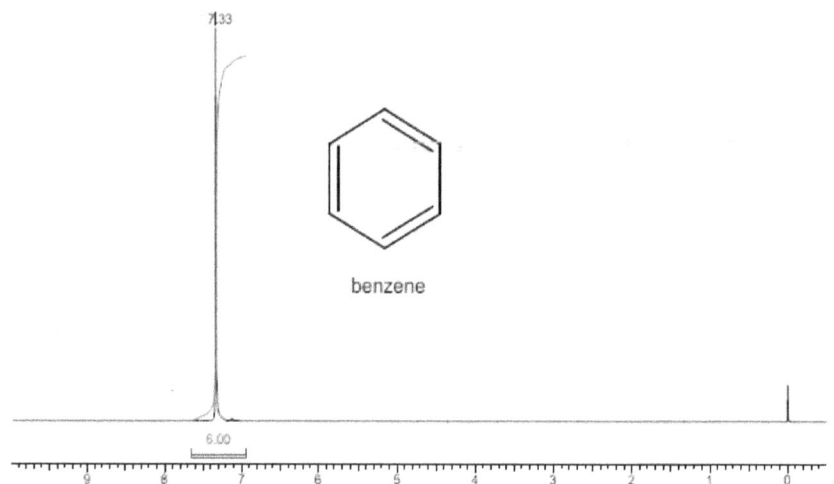

benzene

If a hydrogen atom on the benzene ring is replaced with a different substituent, such as a methyl group, some of the hydrogens become magnetically inequivalent. For example, in the compound toluene, there are three different kinds of hydrogens on the benzene ring. The hydrogens neighboring the methyl (Ha) are magnetically inequivalent to the hydrogens two carbons away from the methyl (Hb) and the hydrogen directly across the ring from the methyl group (Hc). Ha, Hb, and Hc all couple to each other and have J values that correlate with the number of bonds between coupling protons. Ha and Hb are *ortho* to one another (adjacent); Jortho = 6-10 Hz. Ha and Hc are *meta* to one another (two carbons apart); Jmeta = 1-3 Hz. Although there is not an example in this molecule, if two protons are three carbons apart, they are *para*; Jpara = 0-1 Hz. As you can see, the J value decreases as the number of bonds between hydrogens increases. The peak for the aromatic protons is a complex multiplet as a result of the many J values and overlapping peaks. With greater resolution, it is possible to see these separate peaks.

^{1}H NMR of substituted Benzene

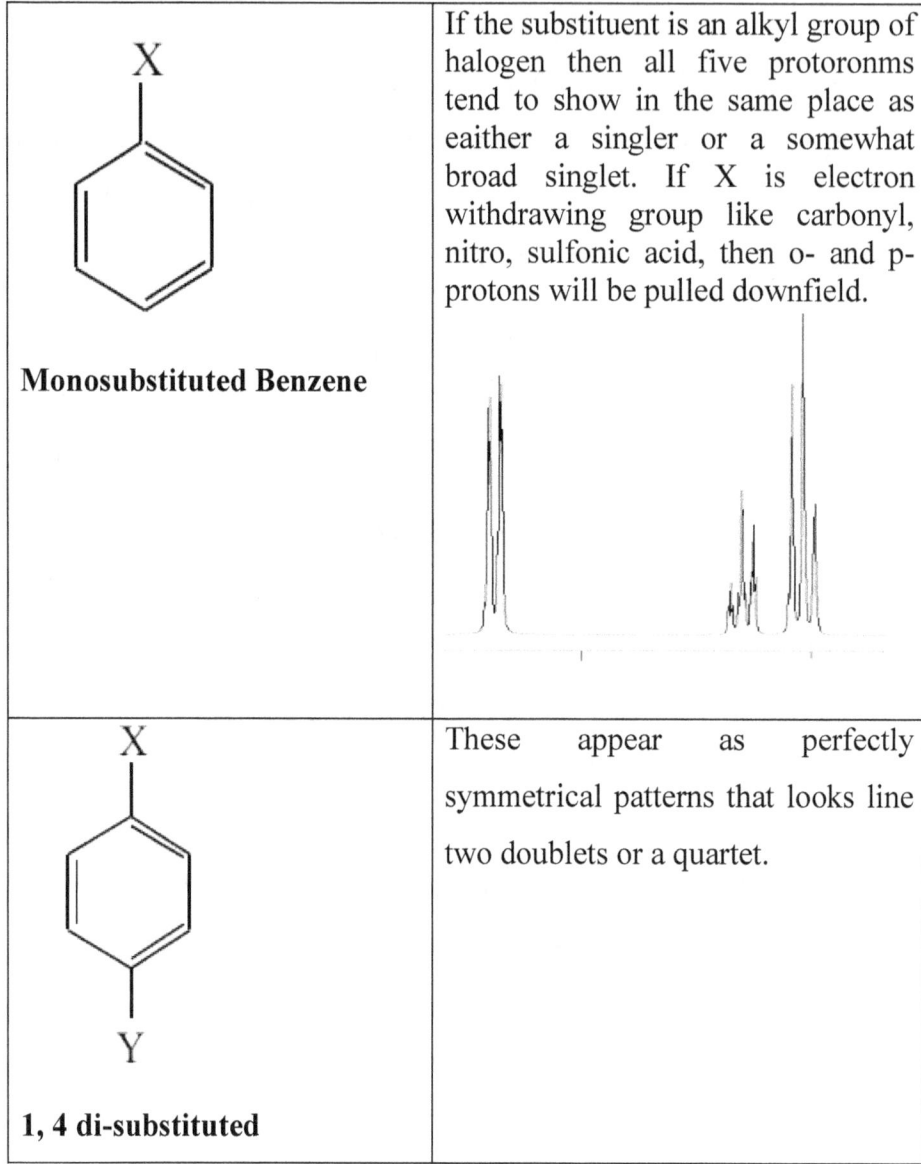 **Monosubstituted Benzene**	If the substituent is an alkyl group of halogen then all five protoronms tend to show in the same place as eaither a singler or a somewhat broad singlet. If X is electron withdrawing group like carbonyl, nitro, sulfonic acid, then o- and p-protons will be pulled downfield.
X ... Y **1, 4 di-substituted**	These appear as perfectly symmetrical patterns that looks line two doublets or a quartet.

NMR SPECTRA OF DIFFERENT COMPOUNDS
NMR Spectra of Ethyl alcohol

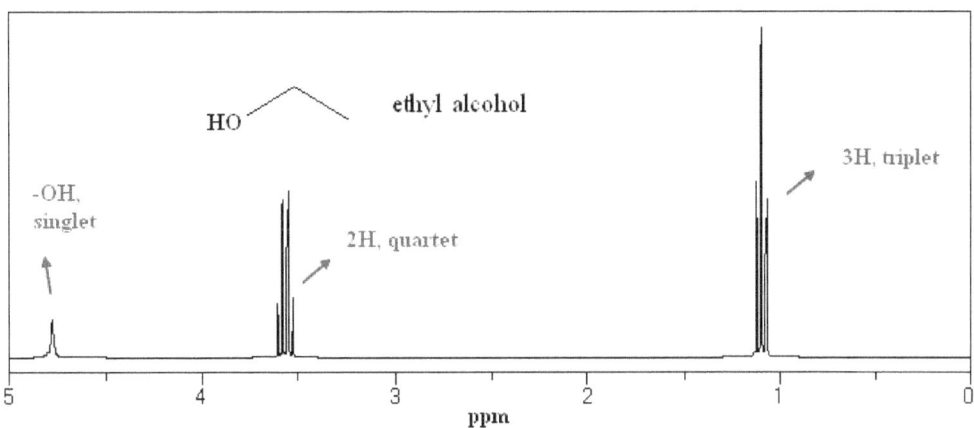

NMR Spectra of 1-propanol

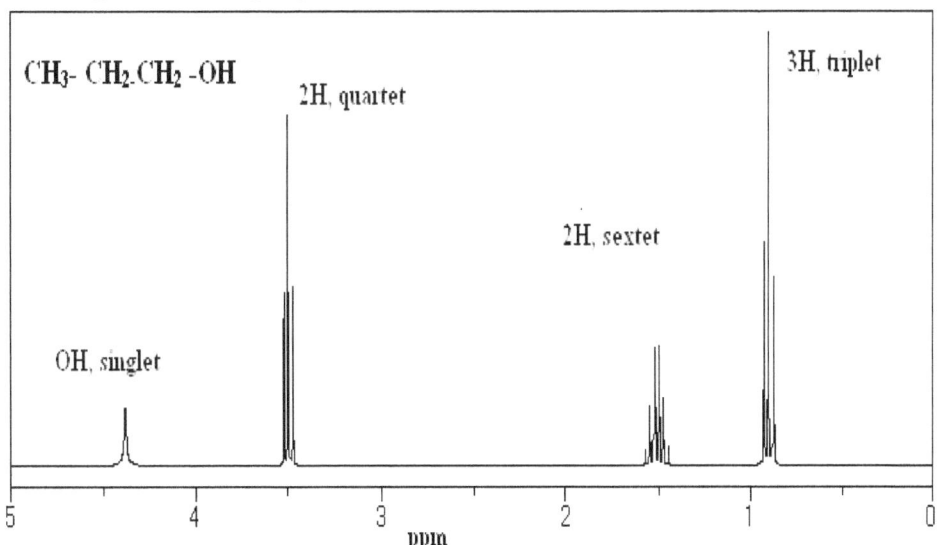

NMR Spectra of 2-propanol

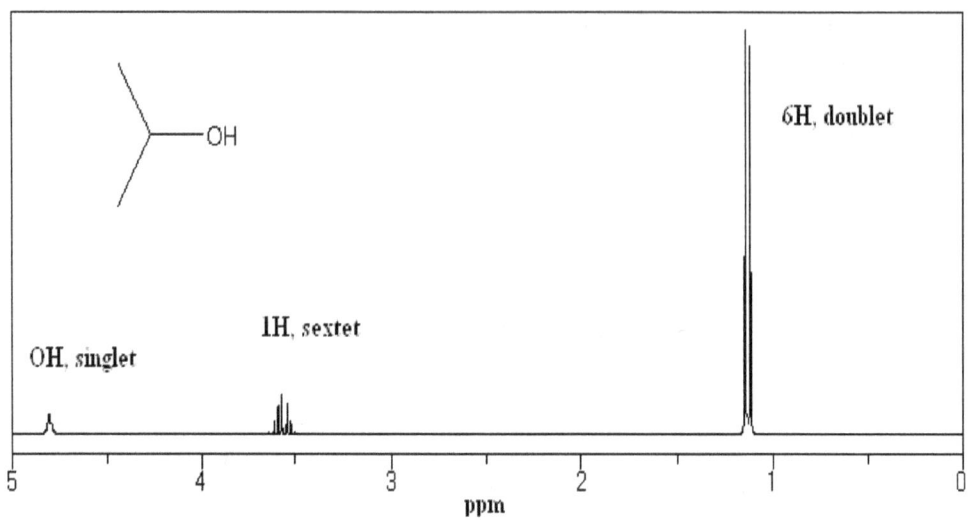

NMR Spectra of 1- Butanol

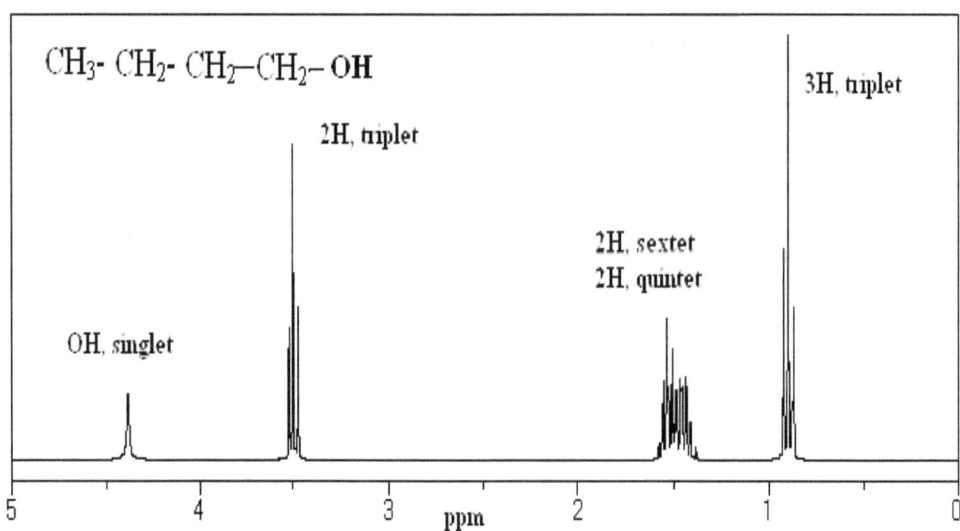

NMR Spectra of 2- Butanol

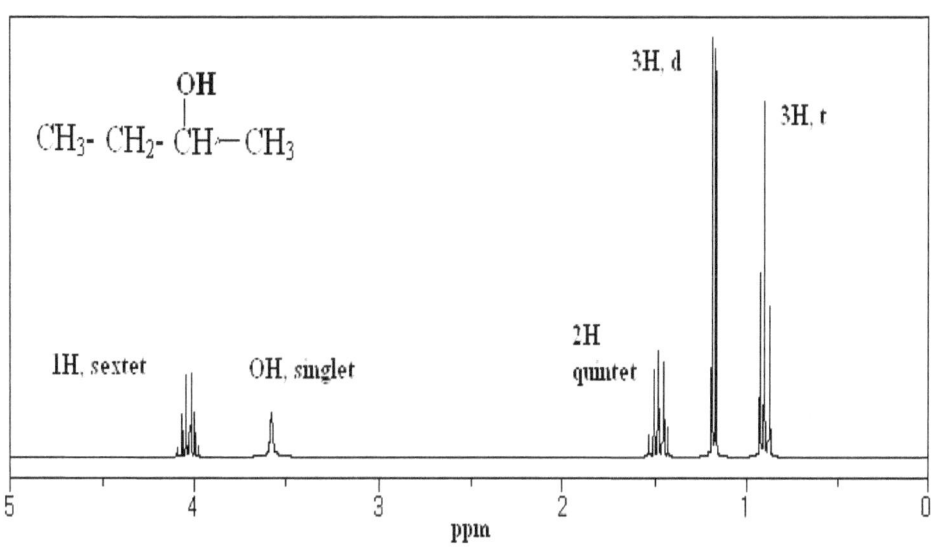

NMR Spectra of 3- methyl-1- butanol

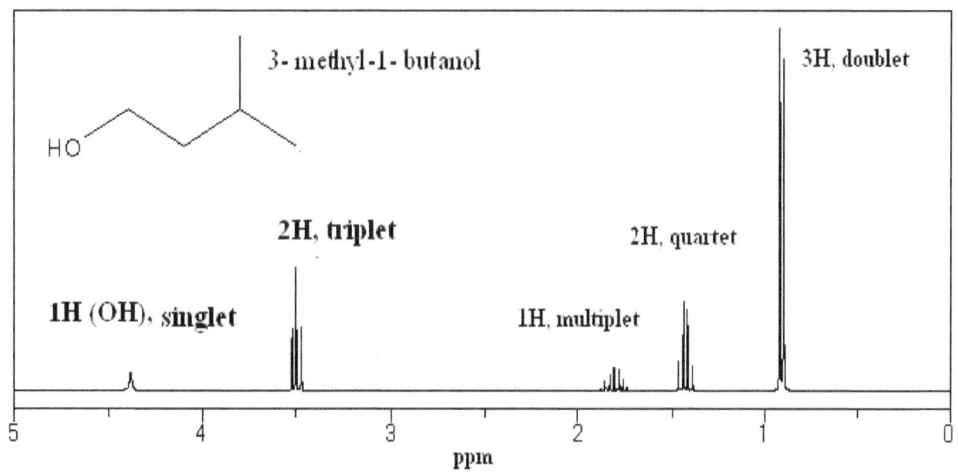

NMR Spectra of 2- methyl-2- butanol

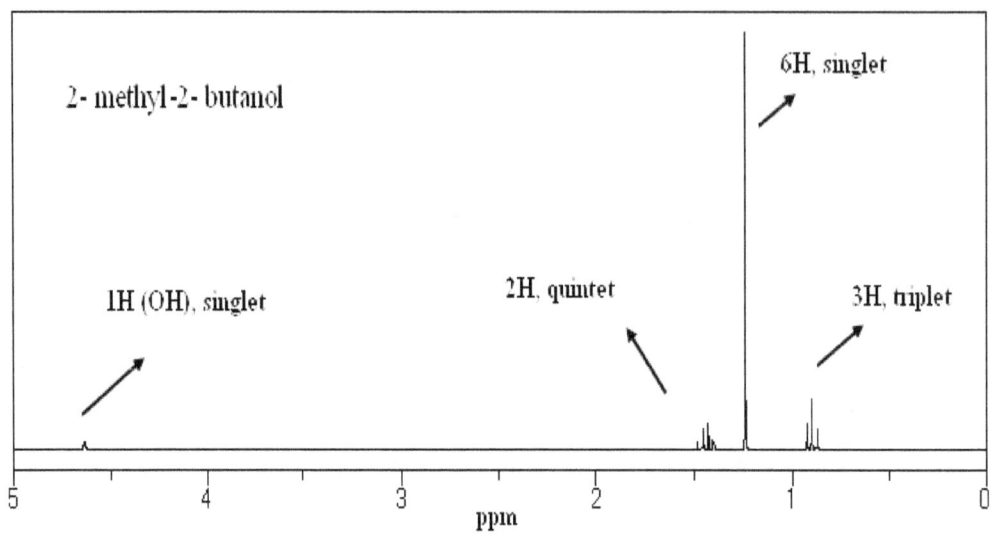

NMR Spectra of 2- methyl phenol

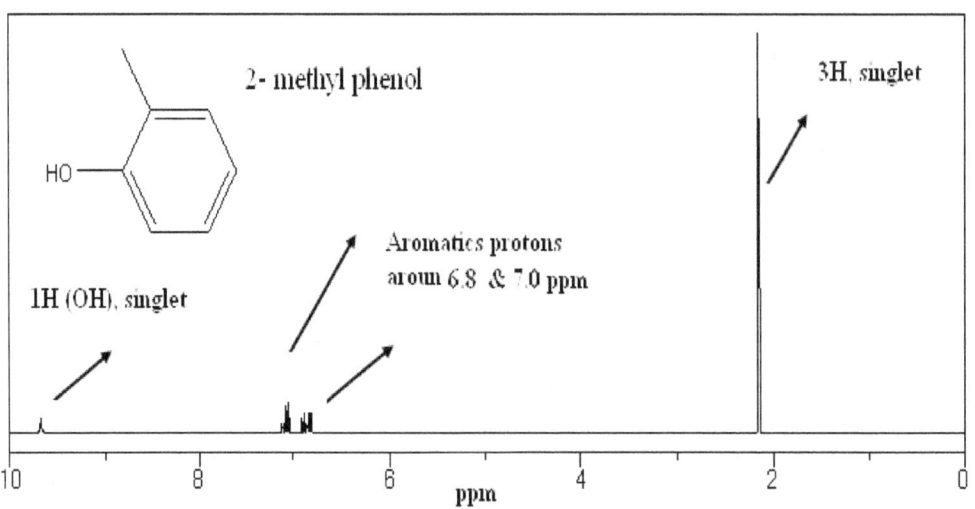

NMR Spectra of 3- methyl phenol

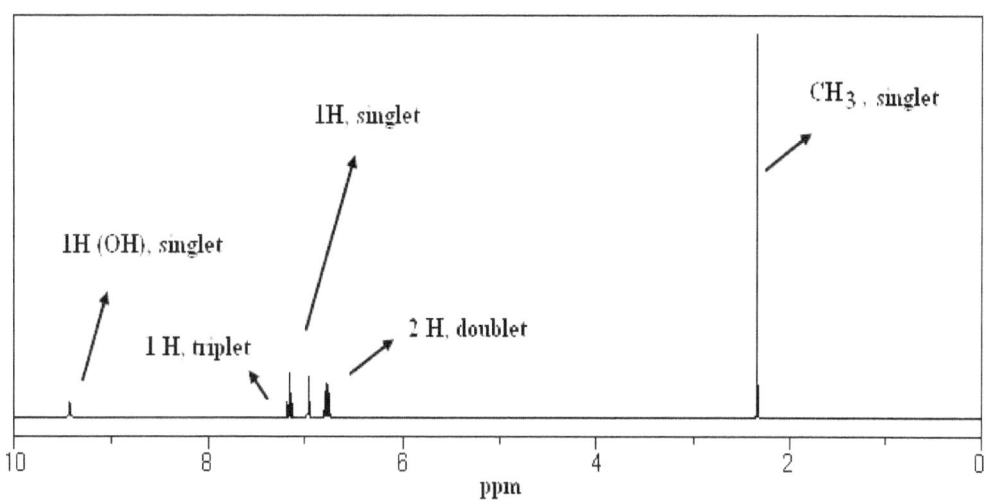

NMR Spectra of 4- methyl phenol

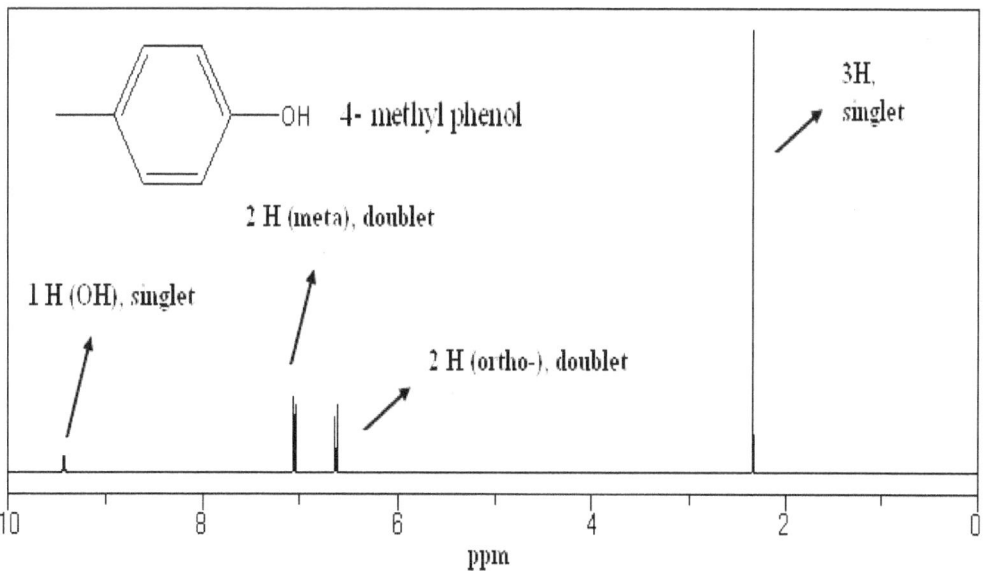

NMR Spectra of 2-ethyl phenol

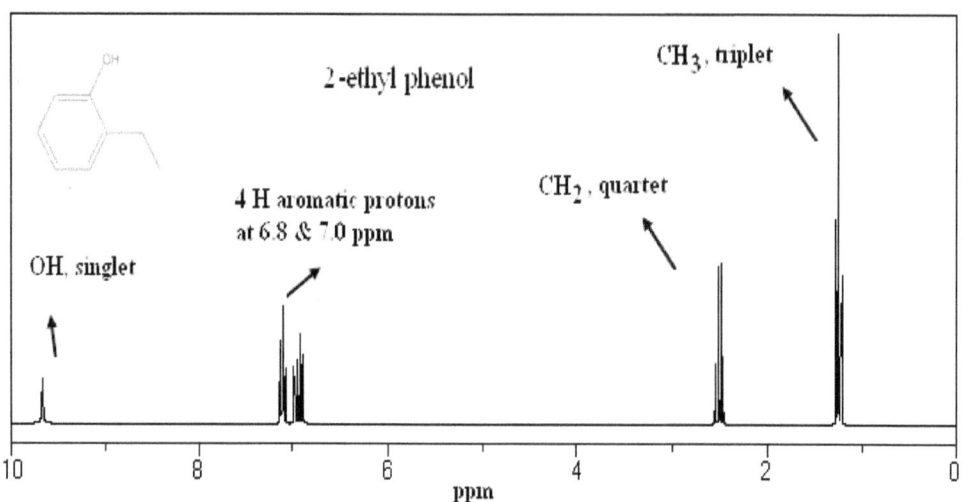

NMR Spectra of Propanoic acid

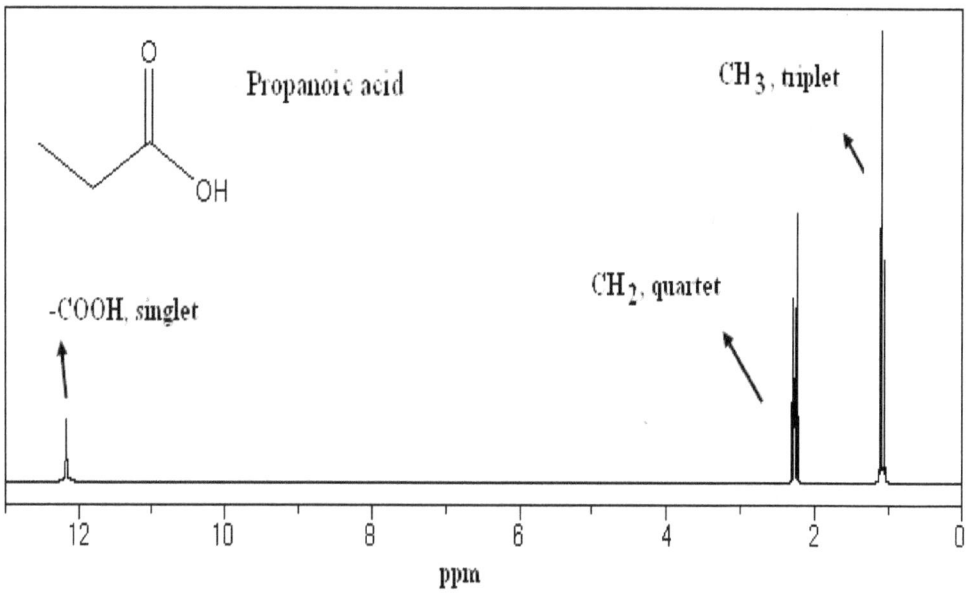

NMR Spectra of Butanoic acid

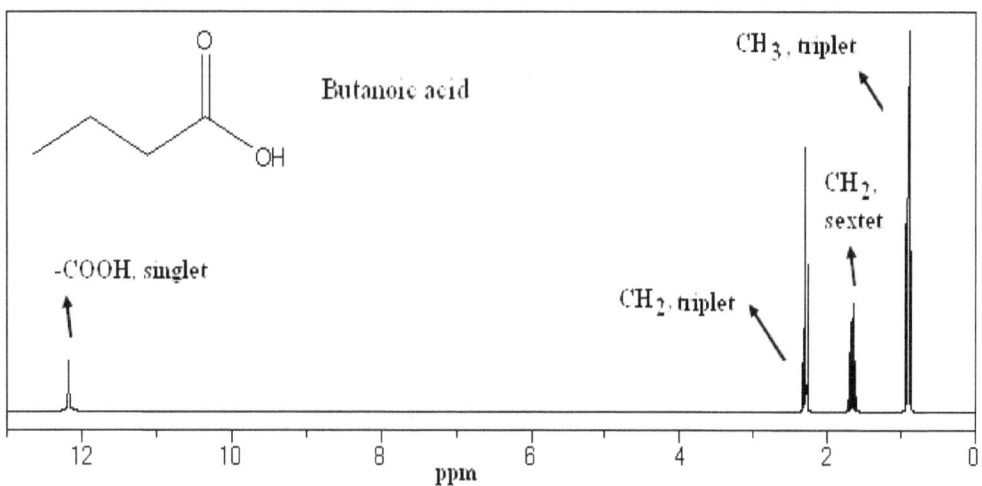

NMR Spectra of Propandioic acid

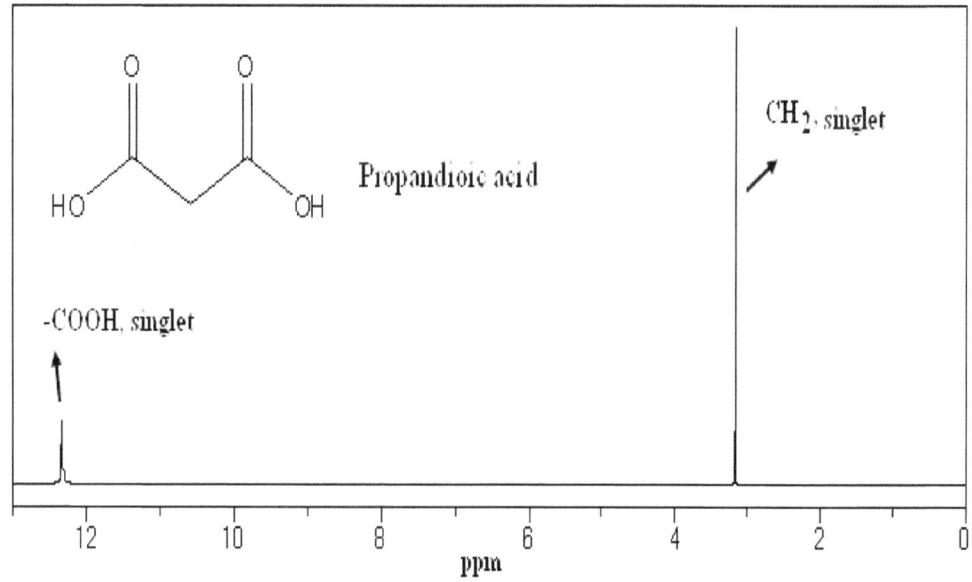

NMR Spectra of Butandioic acid

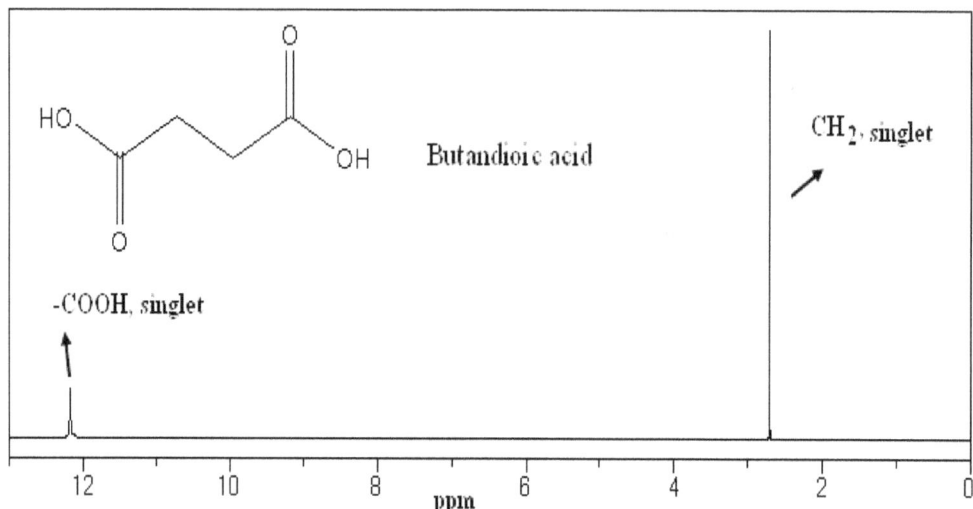

NMR Spectra of Pentandioic acid

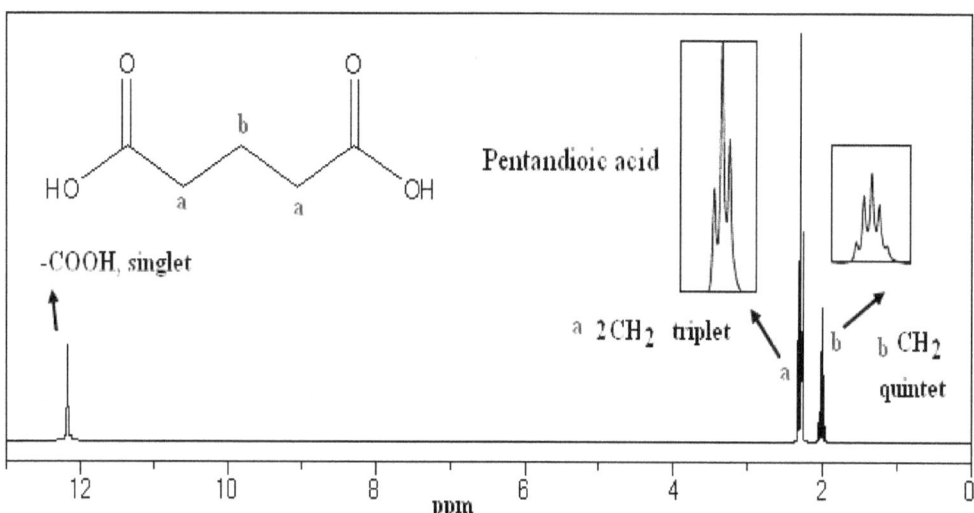

NMR Spectra of hexanedioic acid

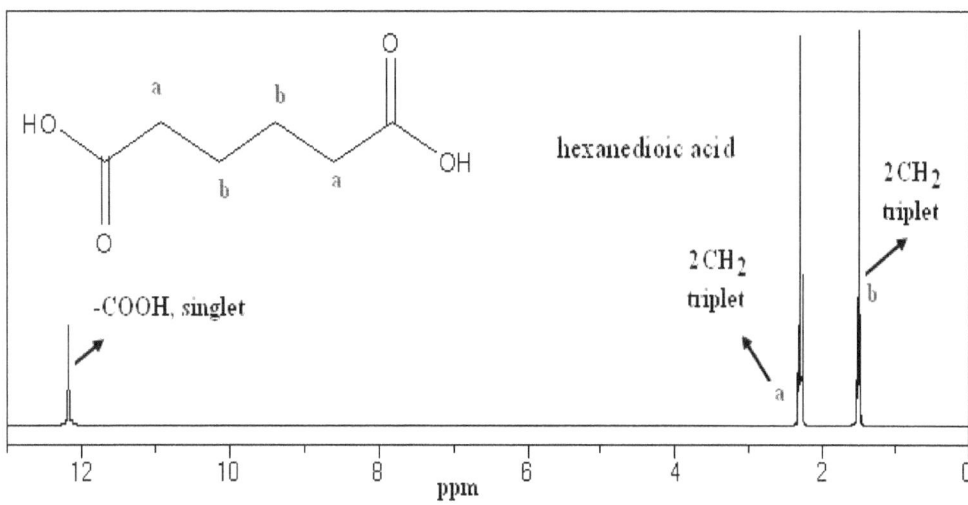

NMR Spectra of Benzoic acid

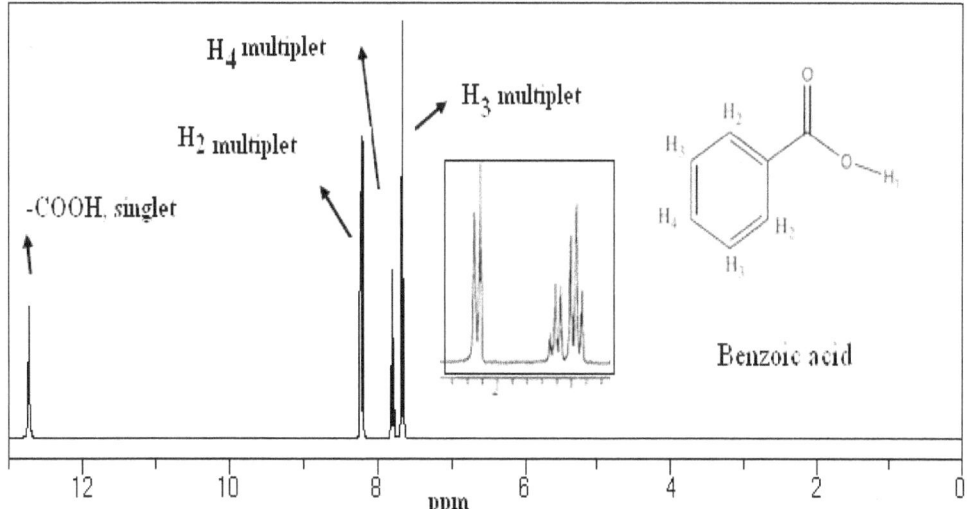

NMR Spectra of 2-methylbenzoic acid

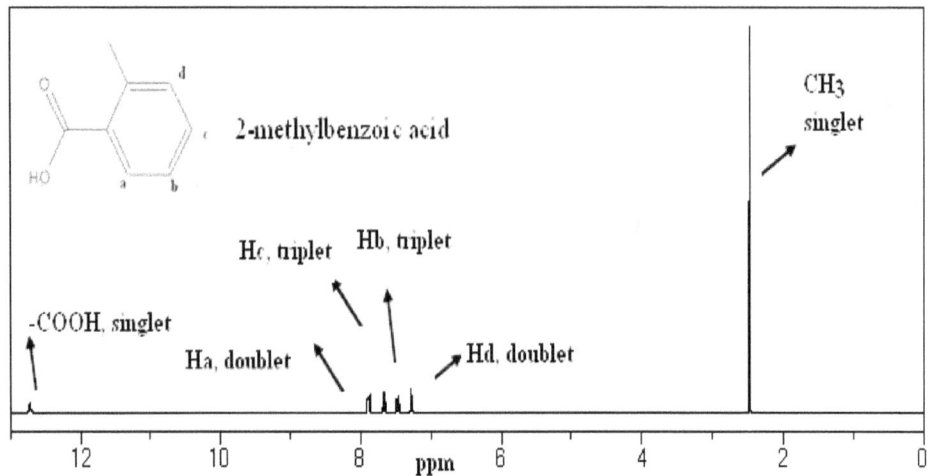

NMR Spectra of pentanal

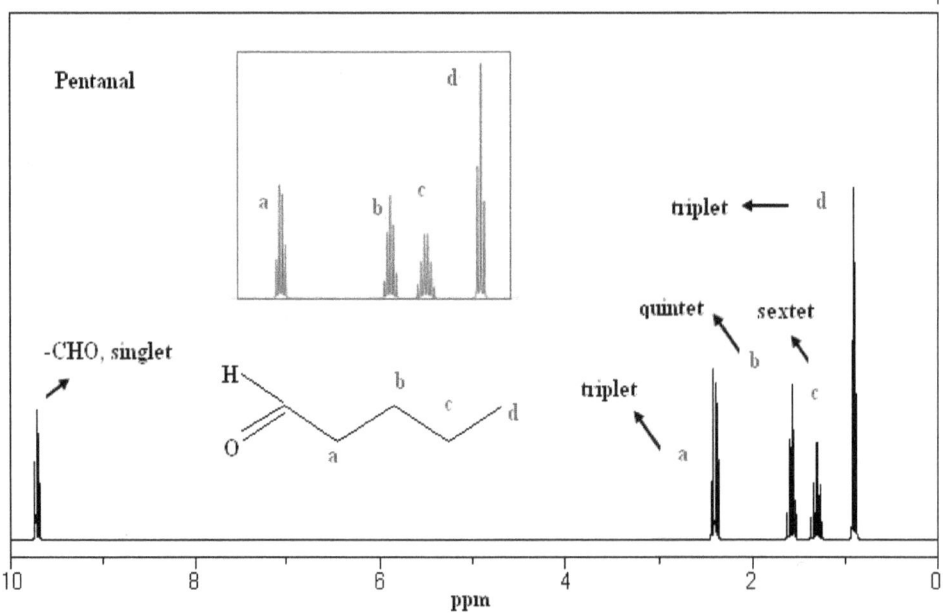

NMR Spectra of Benzaldehyde

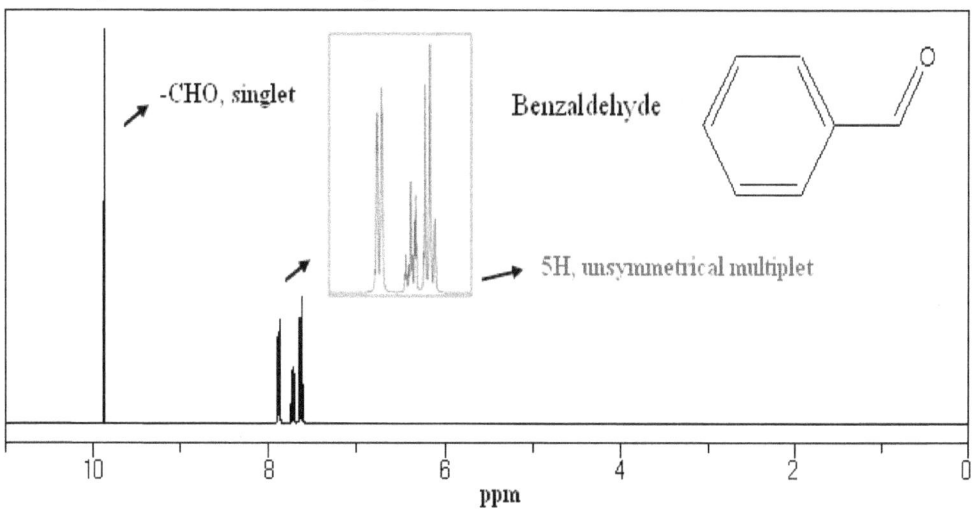

NMR Spectra of 2-hydroxybenzaldehyde

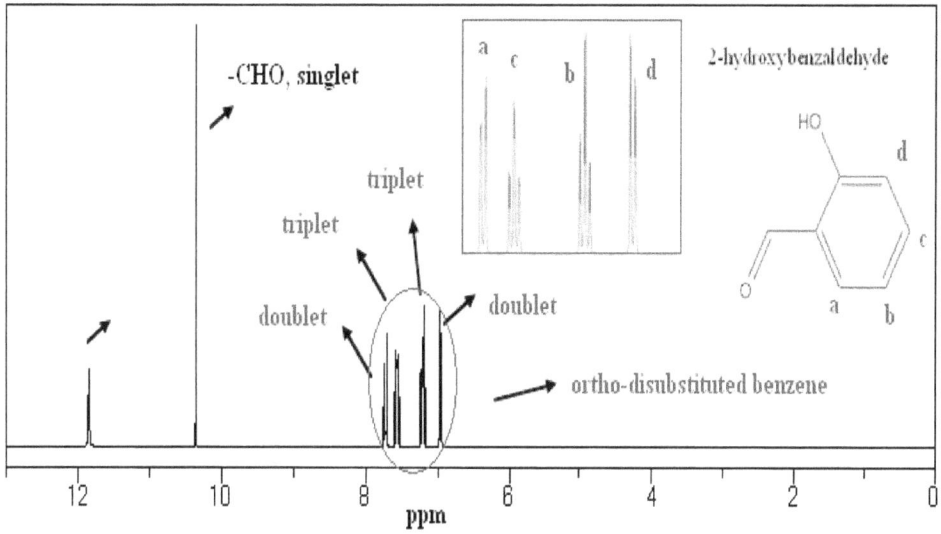

NMR Spectra of 3-hydroxybenzaldehyde

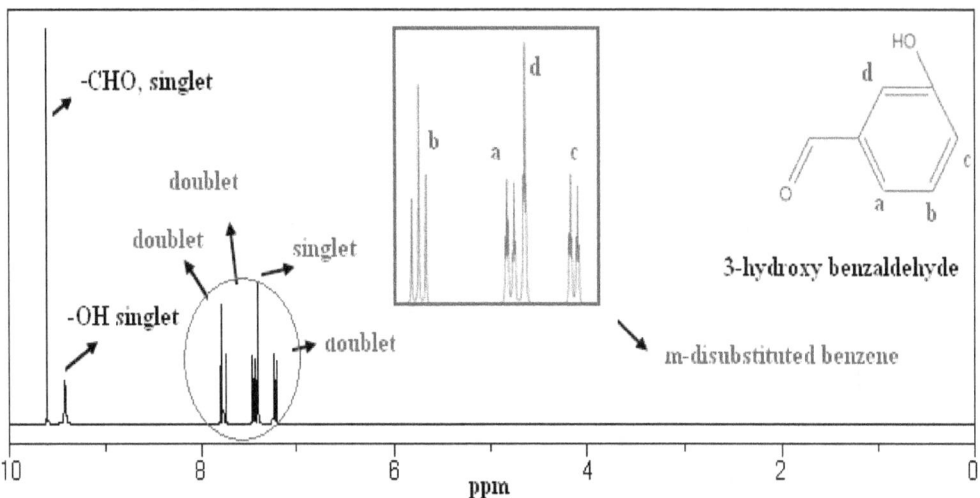

NMR Spectra of 2,4-dichlorobenzaldehyde

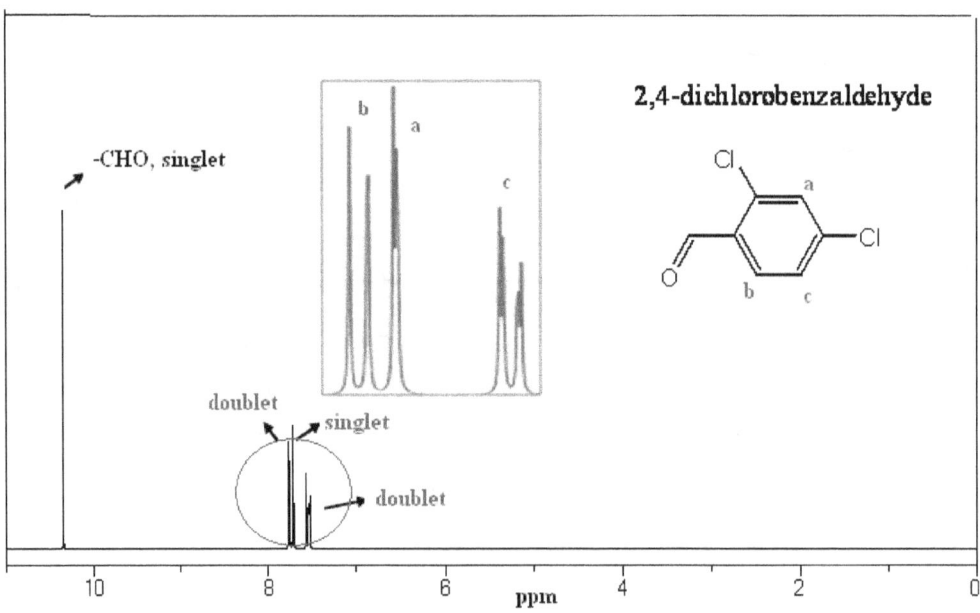

NMR Spectra of 2-propanone

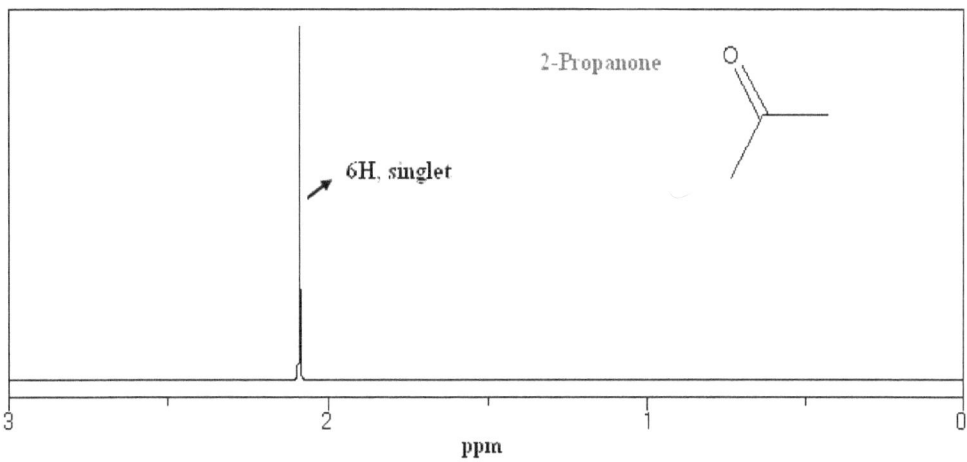

NMR Spectra of Butanone

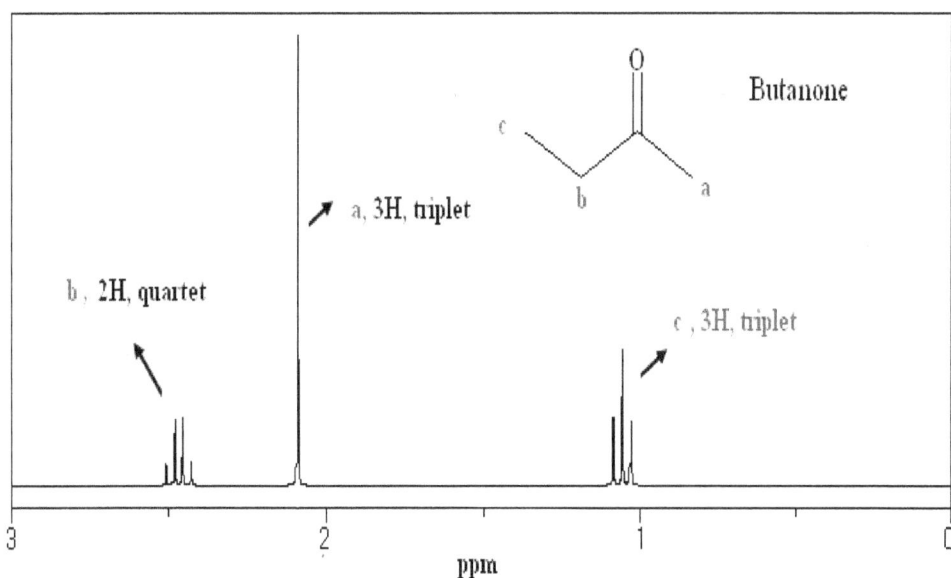

NMR Spectra of 2-pentanone

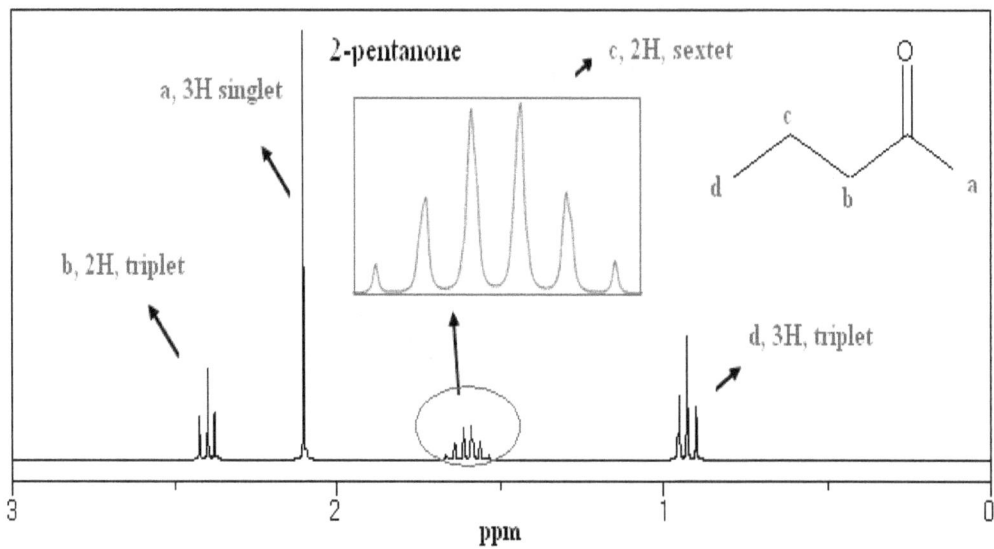

NMR Spectra of 3-pentanone

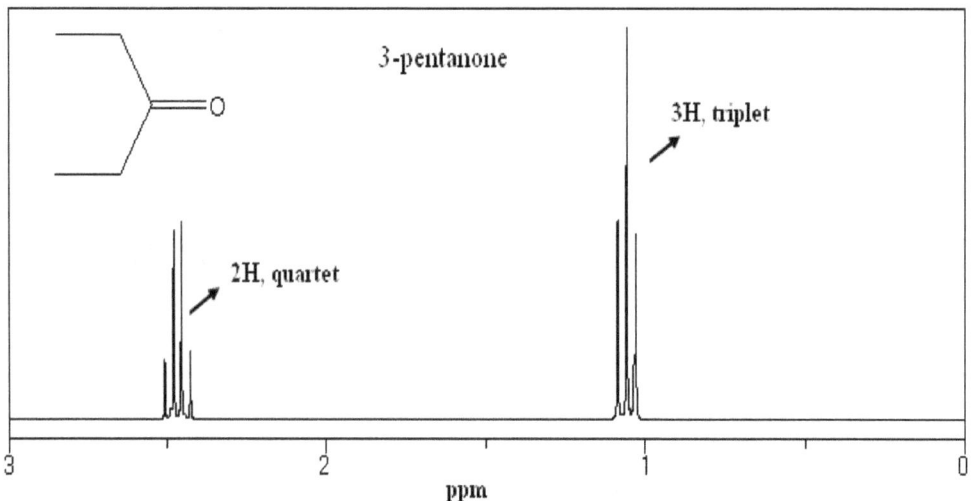

NMR Spectra of 3-heptanone

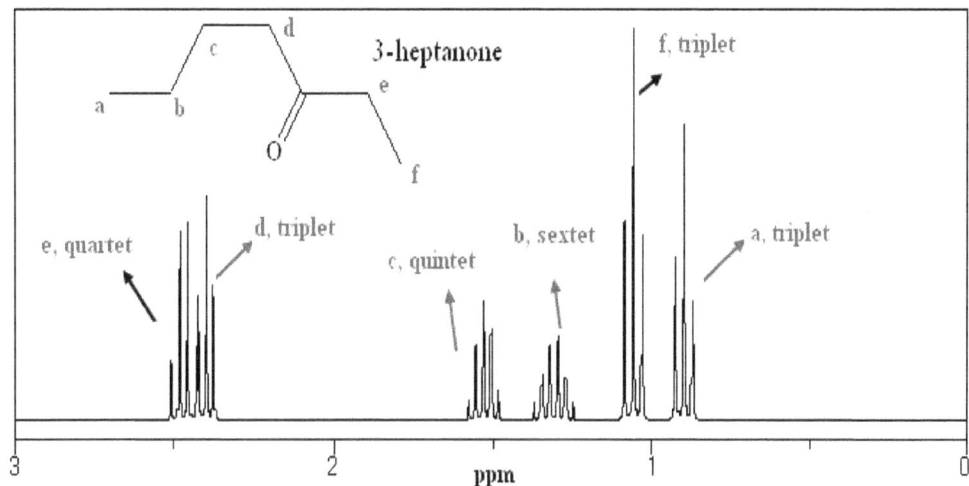

NMR Spectra of Butylamine

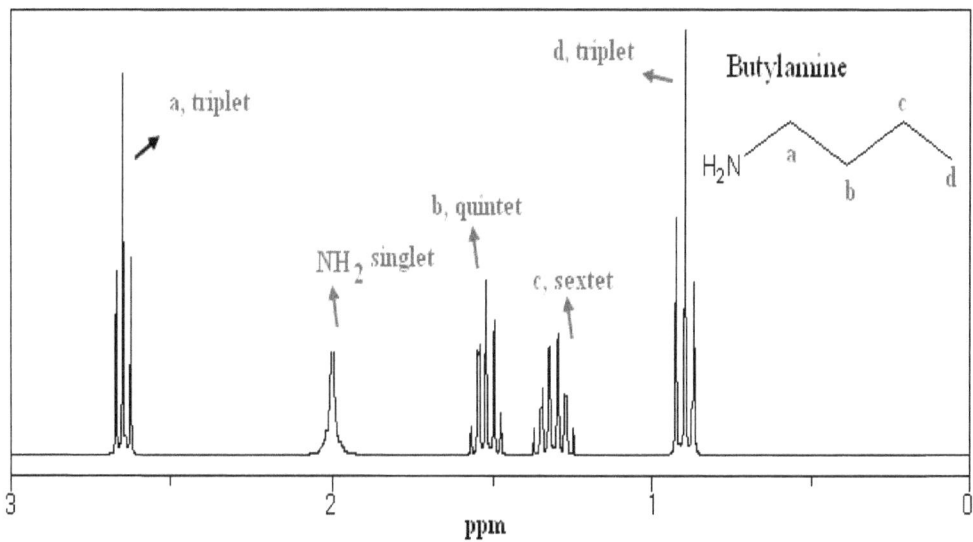

NMR Spectra of Sec-Butylamine

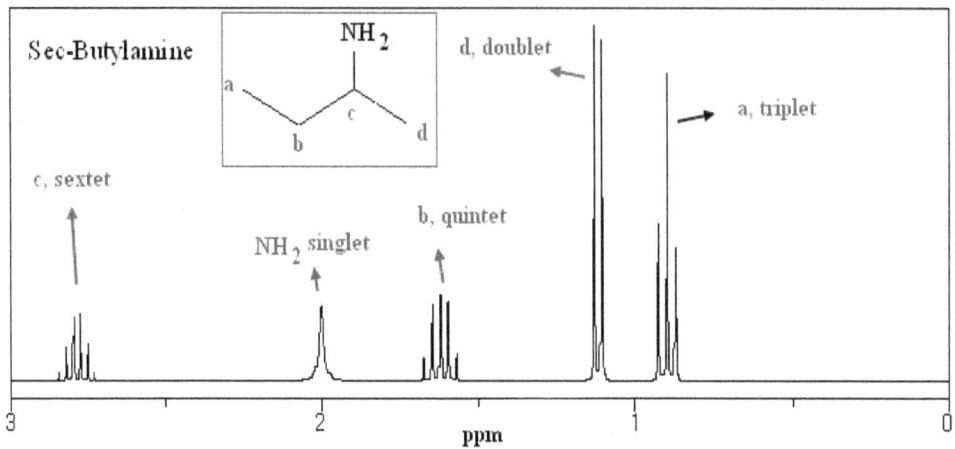

NMR Spectra of Benzamide

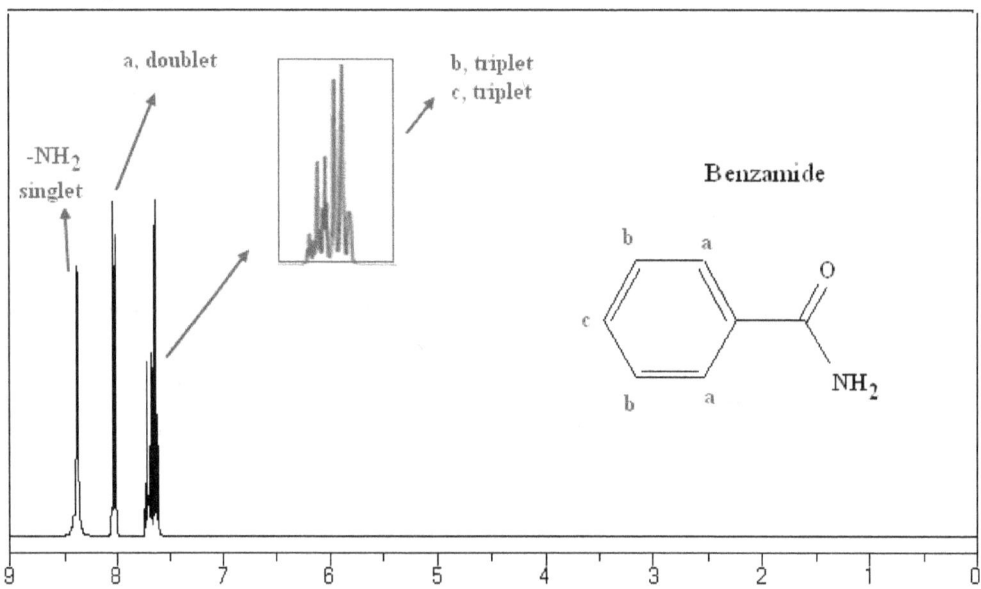

NMR Spectra of N-Phenylacetamide

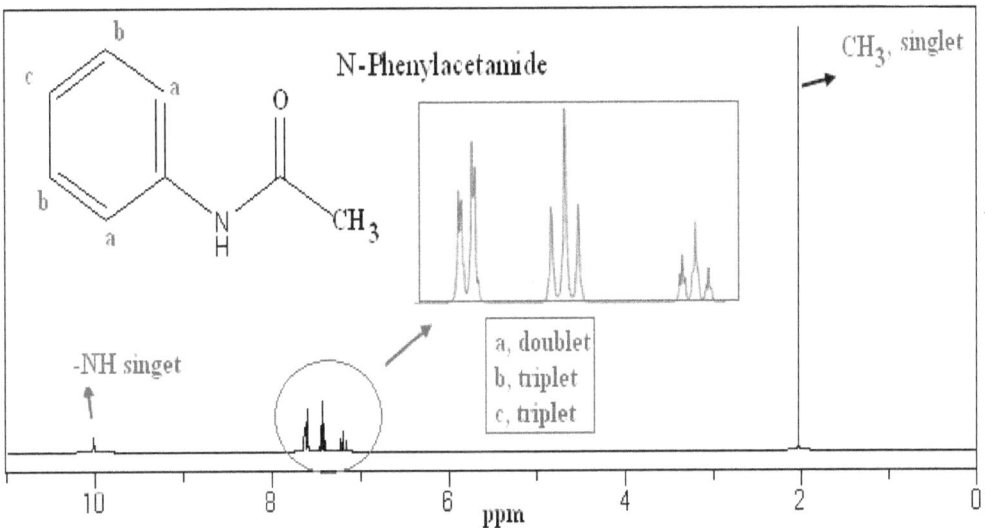

NMR Spectra of Aniline

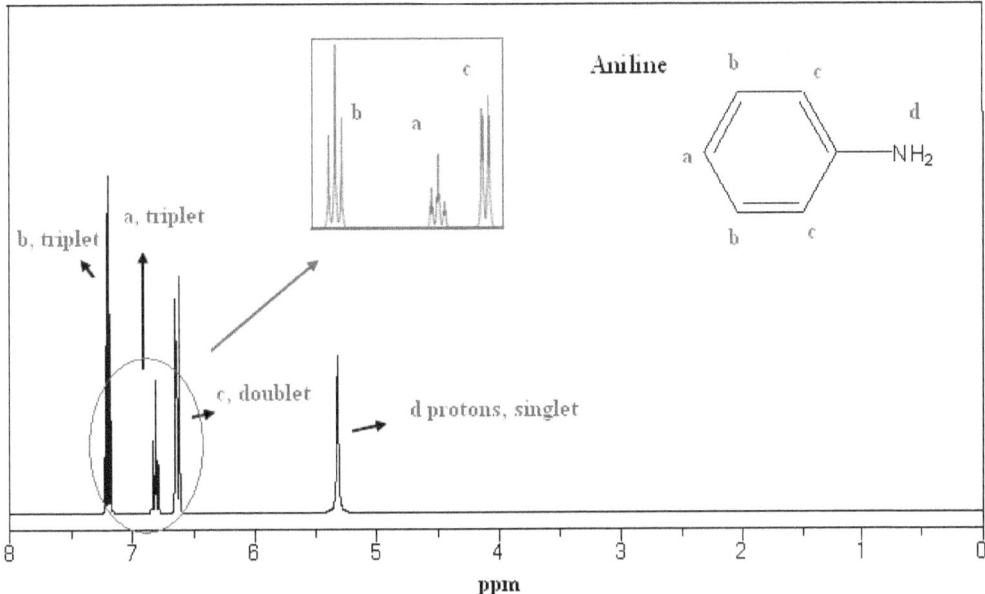

NMR Spectra of Crotonaldehyde

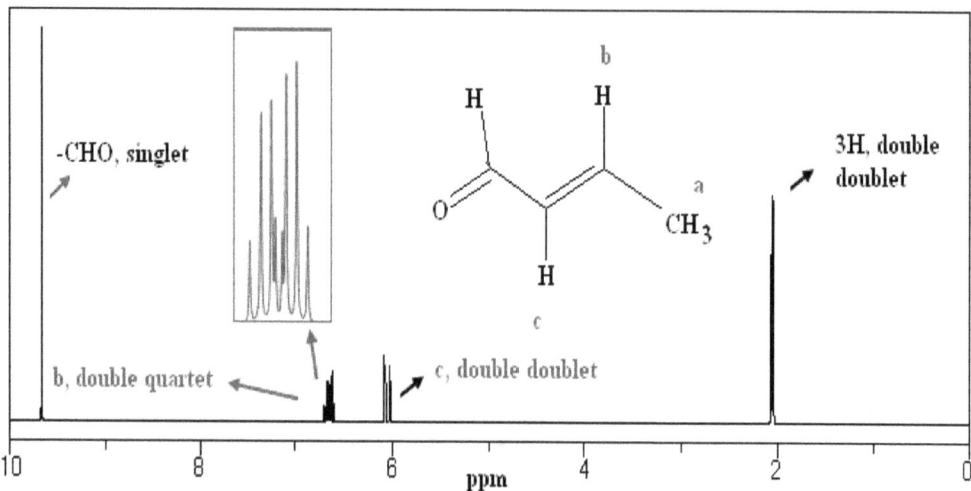

NMR Spectra of Pentane

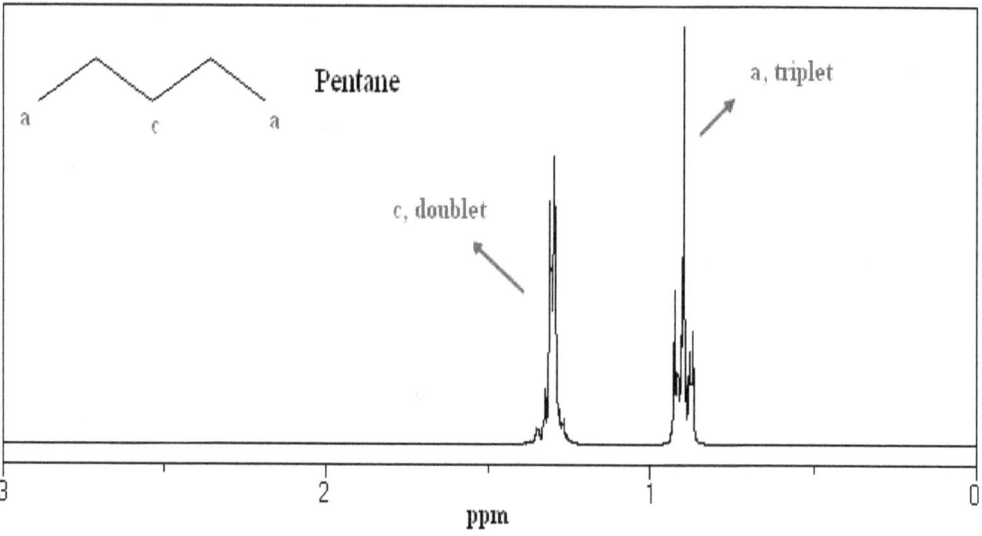

108

NMR Spectra of Pentene

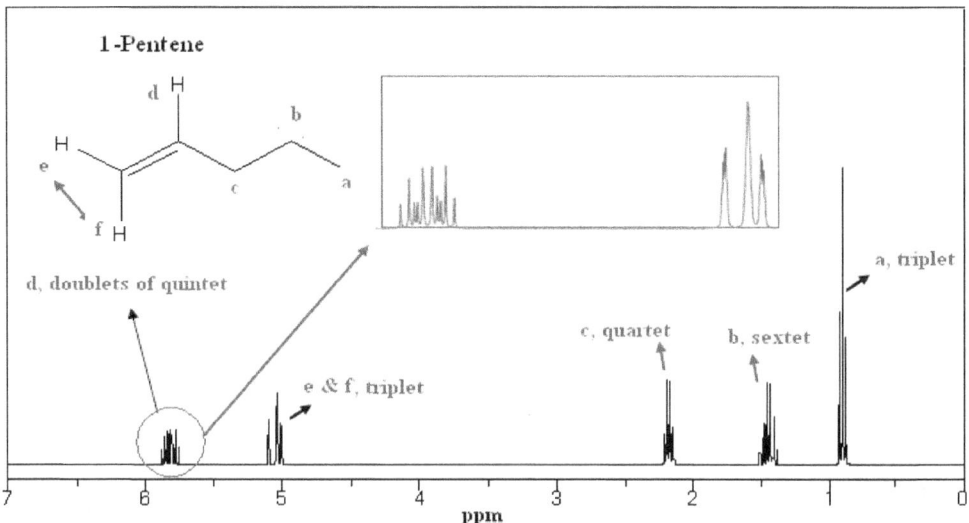

1-Pentene

NMR Spectra of 1-Pentyne

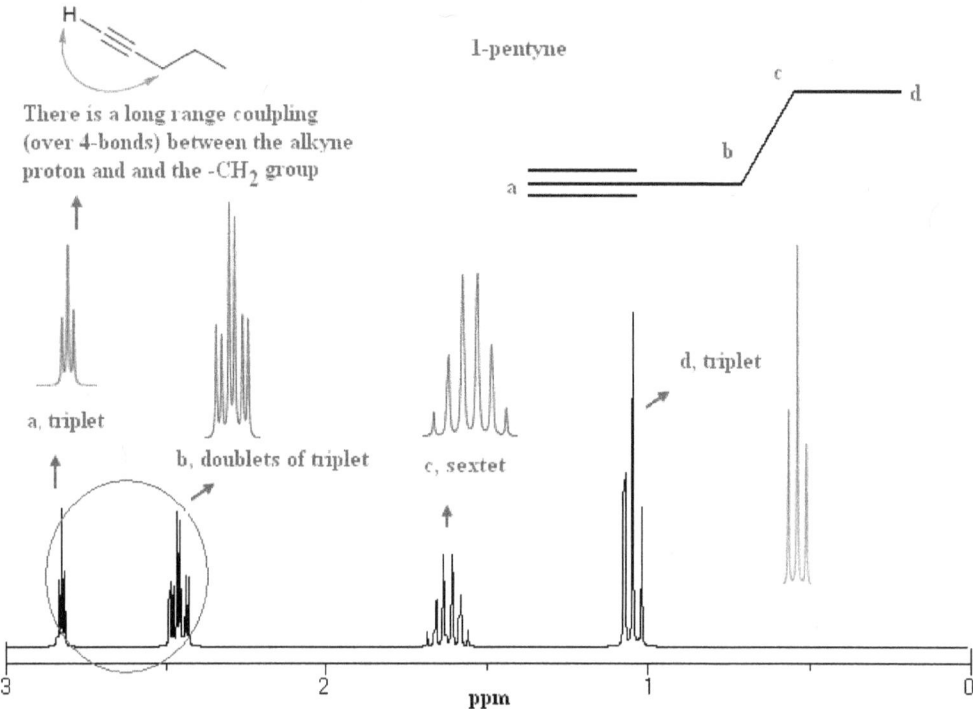

There is a long range coulpling
(over 4-bonds) between the alkyne
proton and and the -CH$_2$ group

1-pentyne

a, triplet

b, doublets of triplet

c, sextet

d, triplet

110

NMR Spectra of 3-heptanone

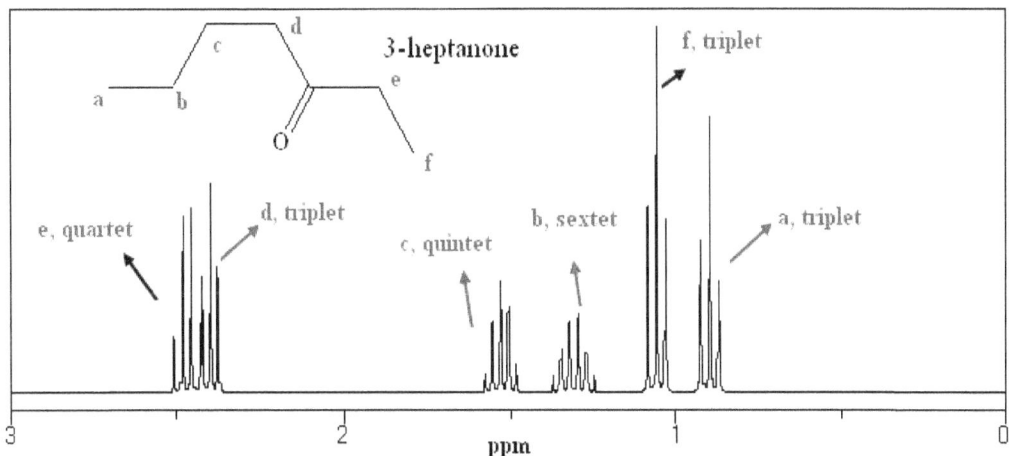

NMR Spectra of Styrene

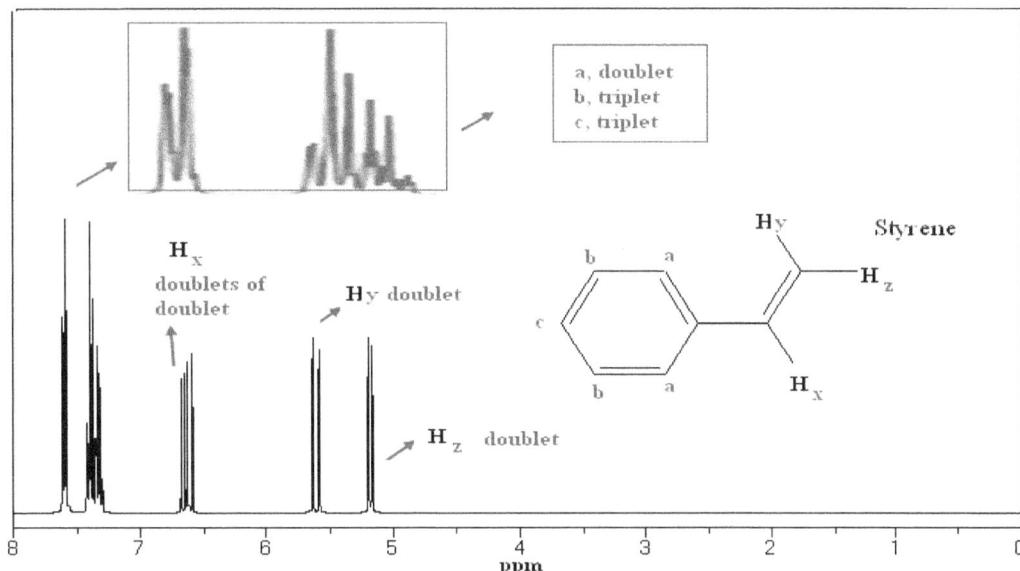

NMR Spectra of 1,2-dimethylbenzene

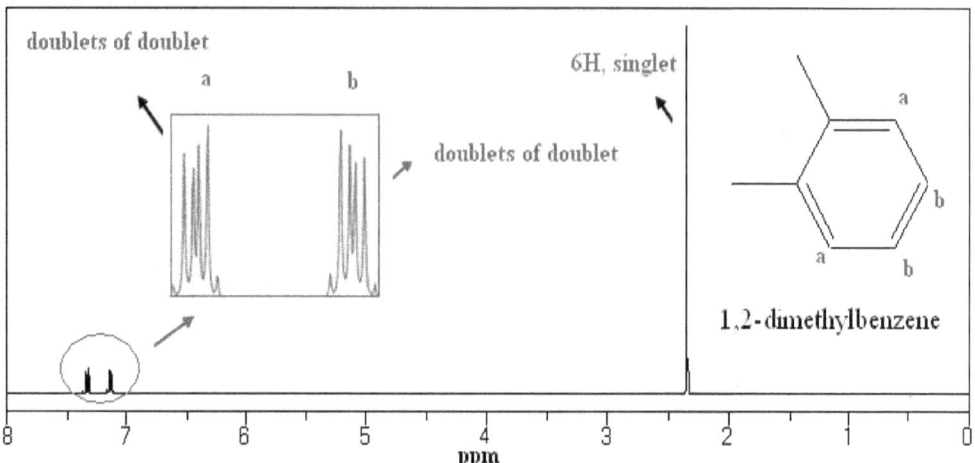

NMR Spectra of 1,3-dimethylbenzene

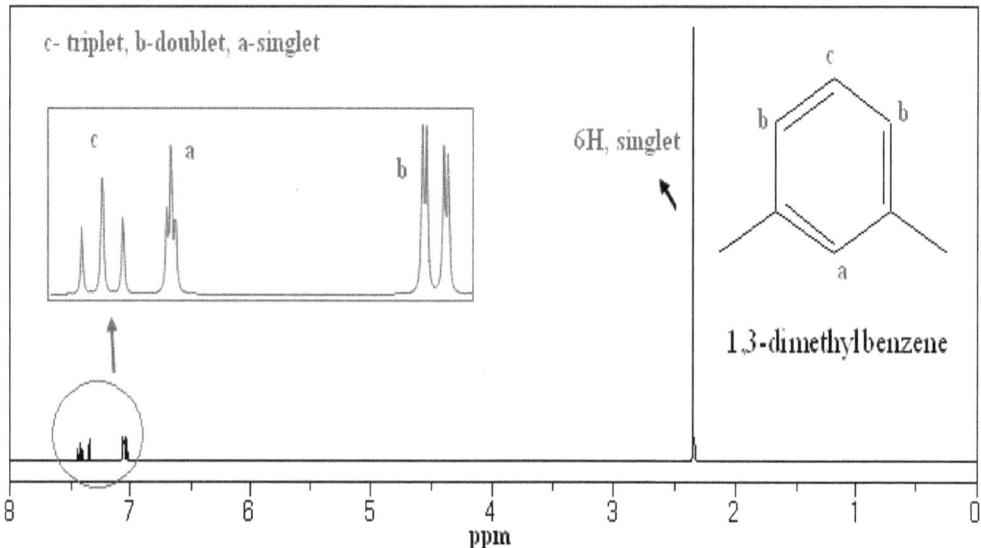

NMR Spectra of Ethyl acetate

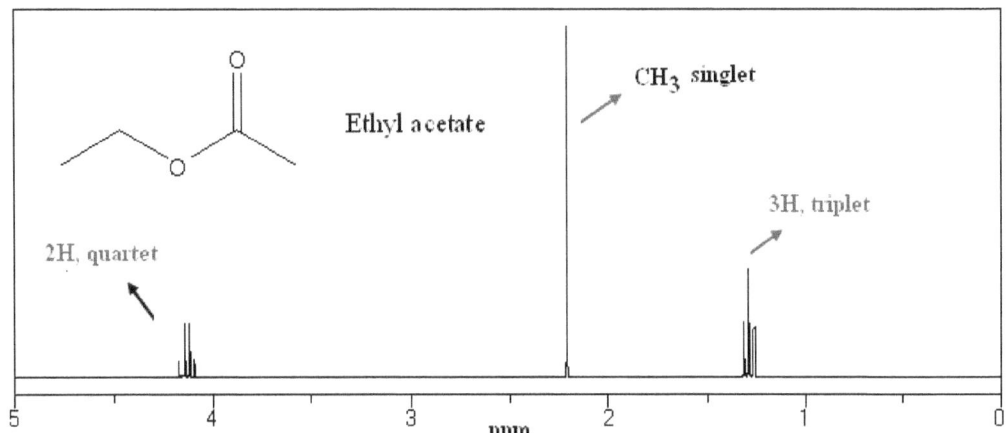

NMR Spectra of Propyl acetate

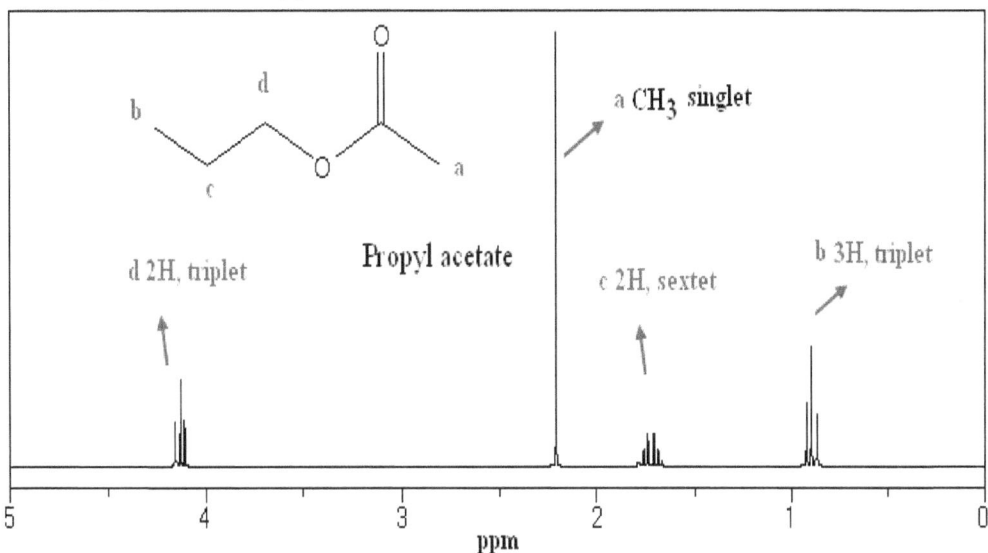

NMR Spectra of Butyl acetate

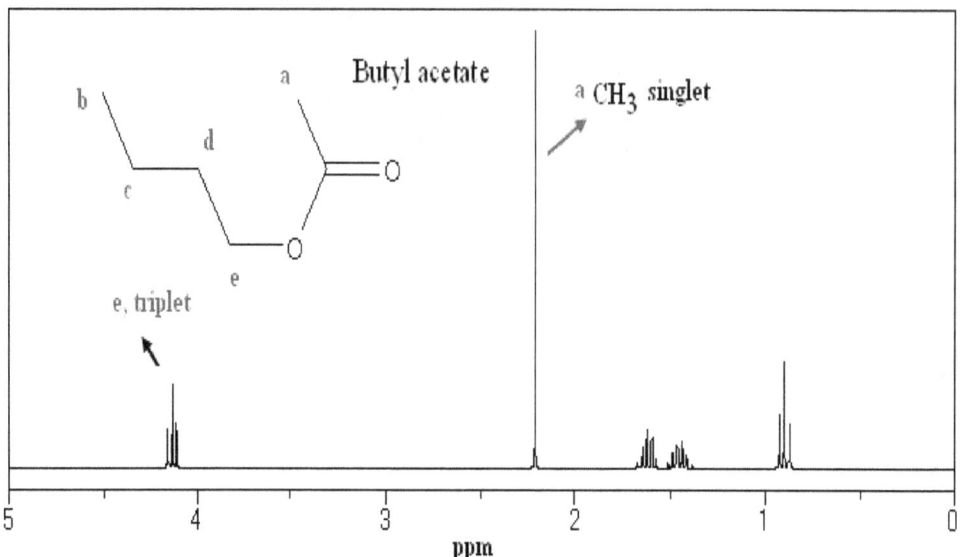

NMR Spectra of Propyl Propanoate

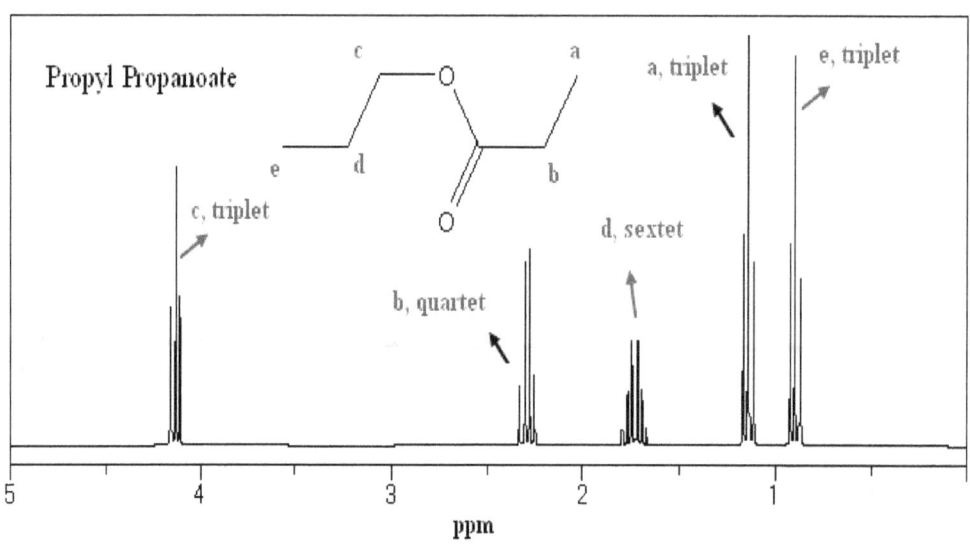

NMR Spectra of Butyl Propanoate

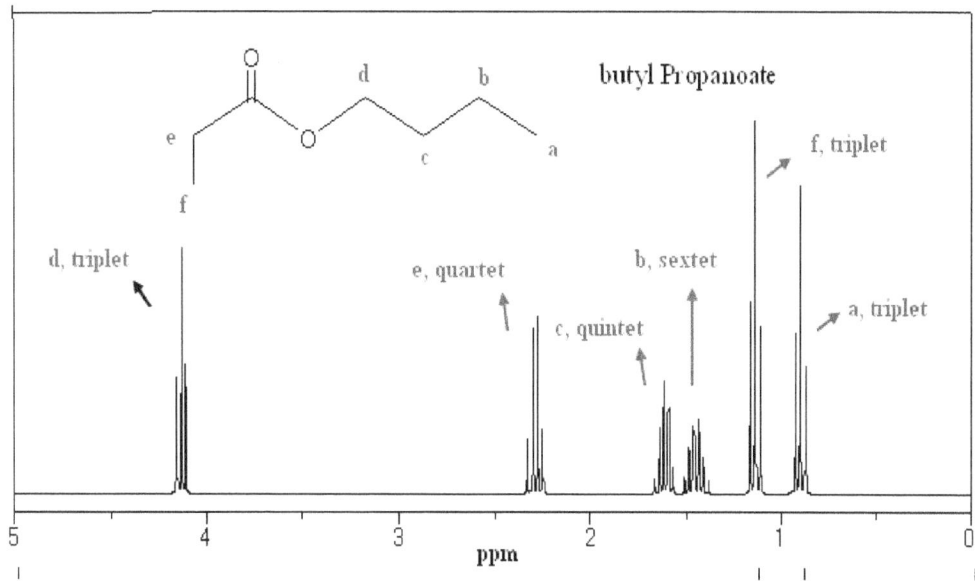

NMR spectra of Diethyl ether

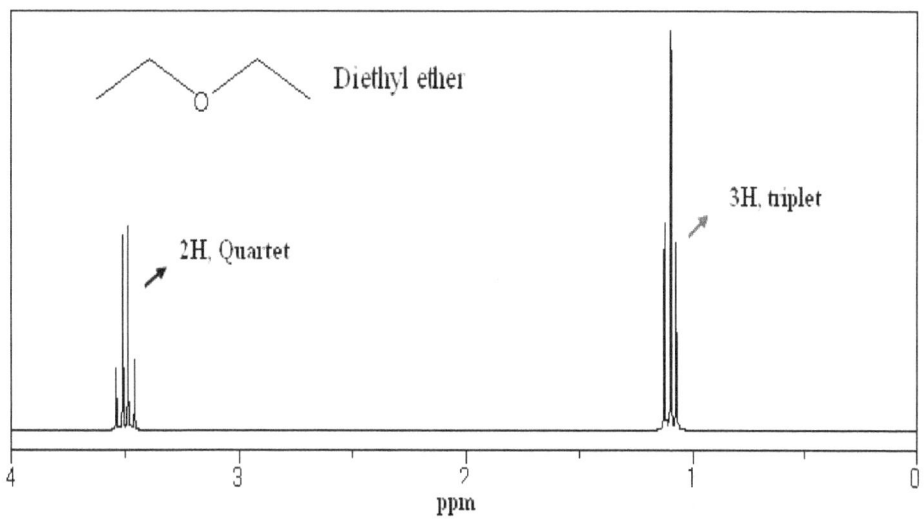

NMR spectra of Diphenyl ether

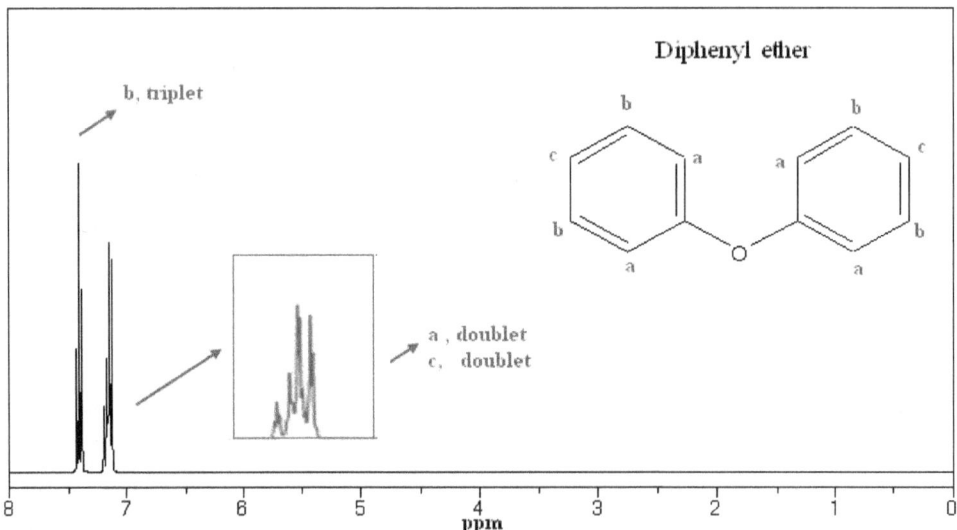

NMR spectra of Tetrahydrofuran

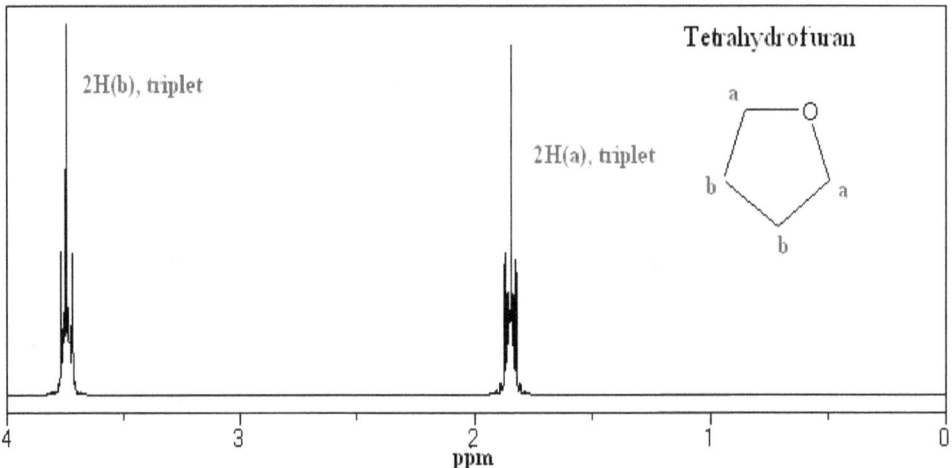

NMR spectra of allyl ether

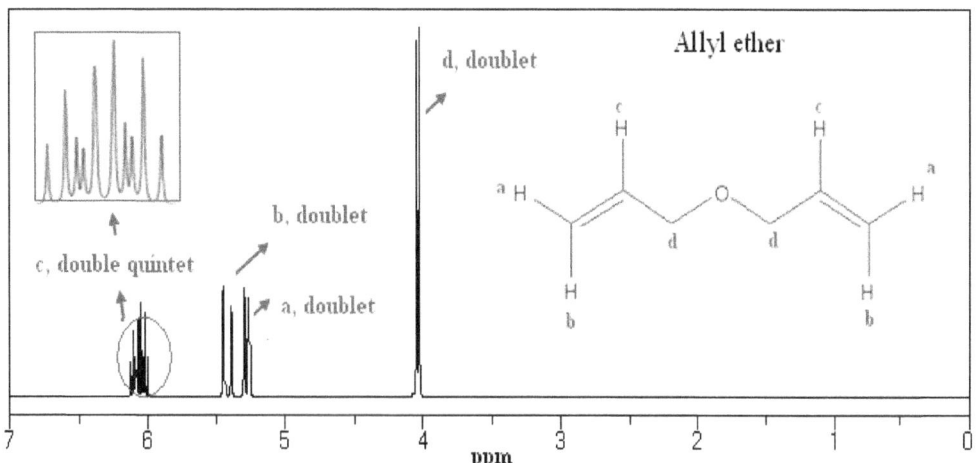

NMR spectra of Acetophenone

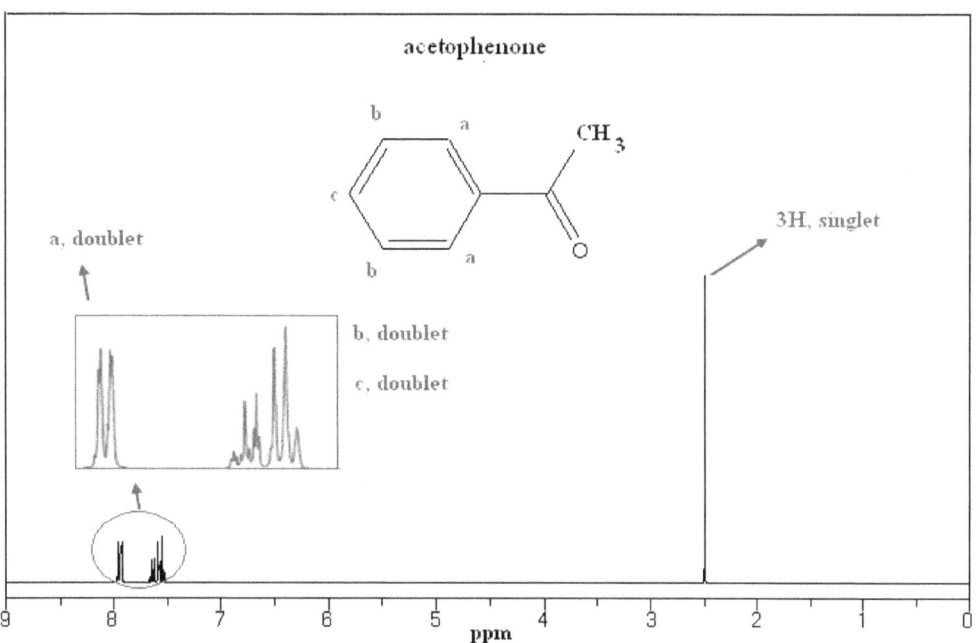

NMR Spectra of given compound

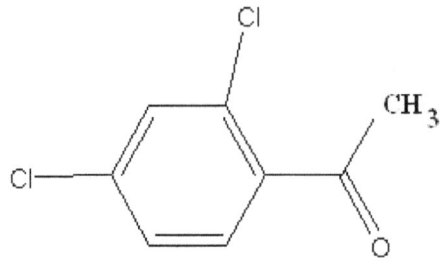

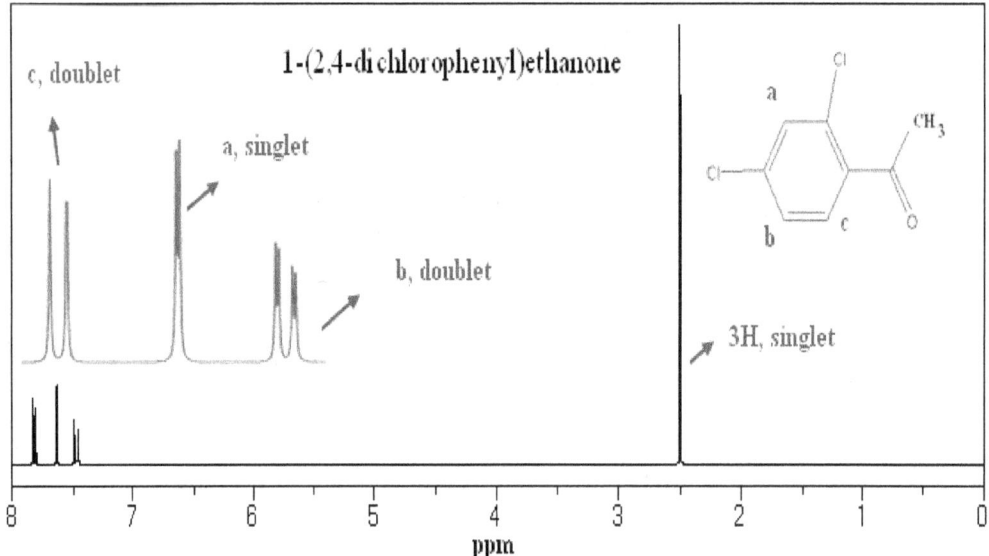

NMR spectra of methacrylic acid

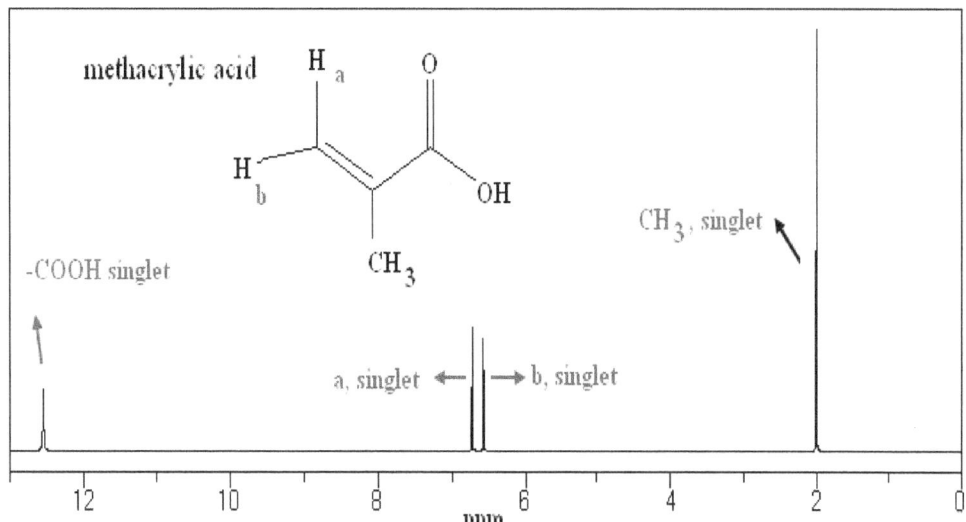

NMR spectra of p-hydroxy benzaldehyde

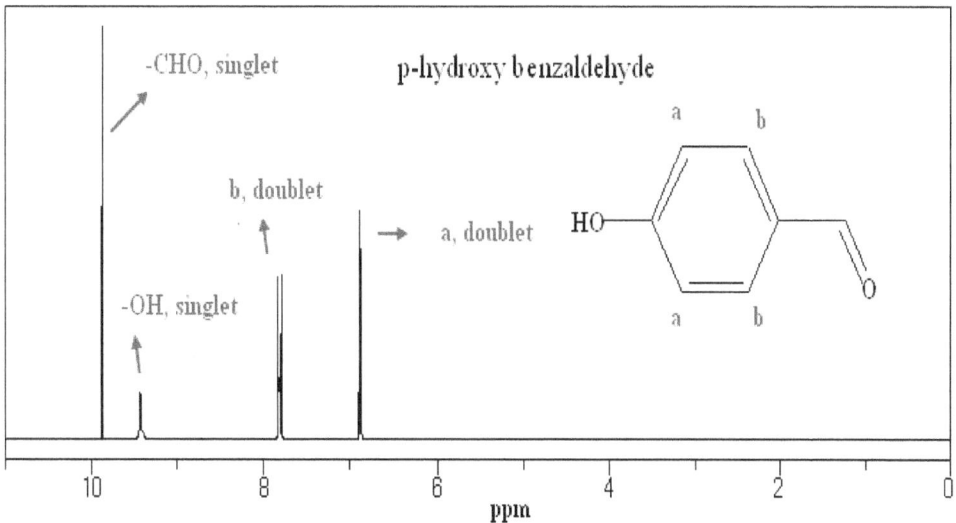

NMR spectra of p-amino benzoic acid

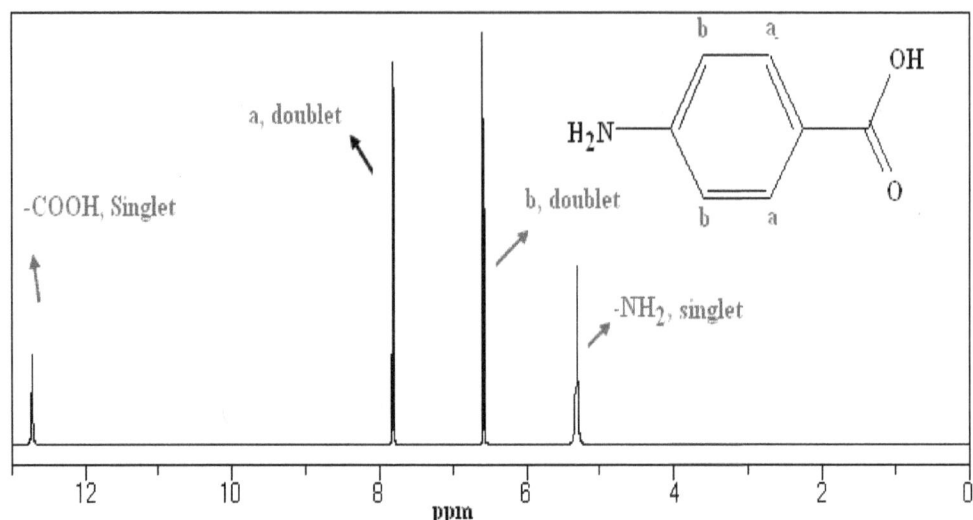

NMR spectra of m-hydroxy benzaldehyde

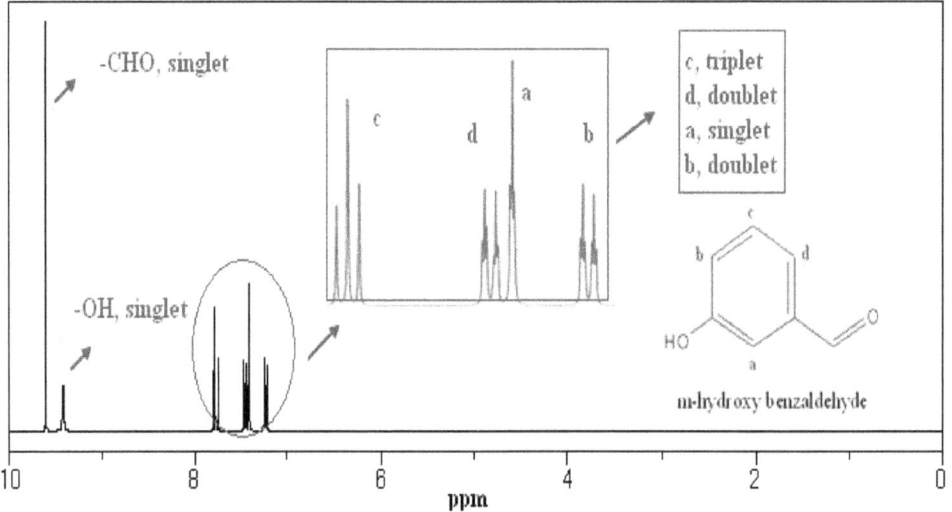

NMR spectra of toluene

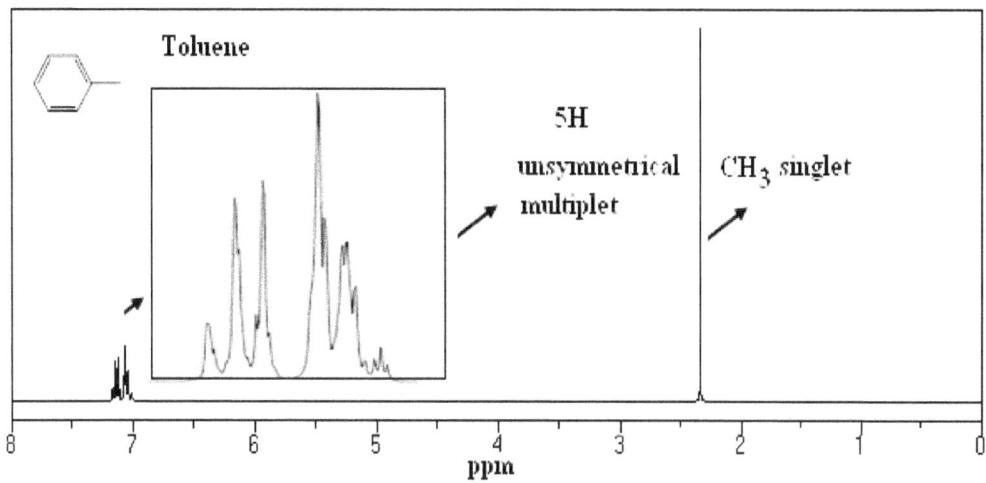

Toluene

5H
unsymmetrical
multiplet

CH$_3$ singlet

QUESTIONS AND ANSWER

1. What is the macroscopic magnetization? Draw the scheme.

It is the sum of all the z-components of all the nuclear magnetic moments in a sample (M0). M0 exists because $N\alpha > N\beta$

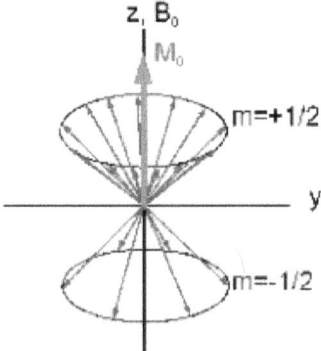

Figur 1: Macroscopic magnetization shown as a sum of vectors.

2. What is the connection between a nuclear angular momentum and a nuclear spin quantum number? Write down the equation.

The nuclear angular momentum is given by the nuclear spin quantum number.

$$P = \sqrt{I(I+1)}\hbar$$

P = Nuclear angular moment

I = Spin quantum number

$\hbar$ = h/2, h = Planck's constant

2. What is the connection between a nuclear angular momentum and a magnetic moment? Write down the equation.

The magnetic moment is proportional to the angular momentum, by the proportionality factor γ. (The magnetogyric ratio is a constant that varies for each nuclide (isotope of a given element). The value of γ determines the sensitivity of the nuclide in NMR, where a higher value means a higher sensitivity.)

$\mu = \gamma P$

μ = Magnetic moment

γ = Magnetogyric ratio

P = Nuclear angular moment

3. Which values can a nuclear spin quantum number have?

0, 1/2, 1, 3/2, 2, 5/2 . . .

4. How many values can the magnetic quantum number have?

The magnetic quantum number m can have the following values: m = I, I - 1, ... ,-IA sum of (2I+1) different values of m.

6. What is the Larmor frequency?

The larmor frequency is the frequency of the precession of nuclear dipoles around the z-axis.

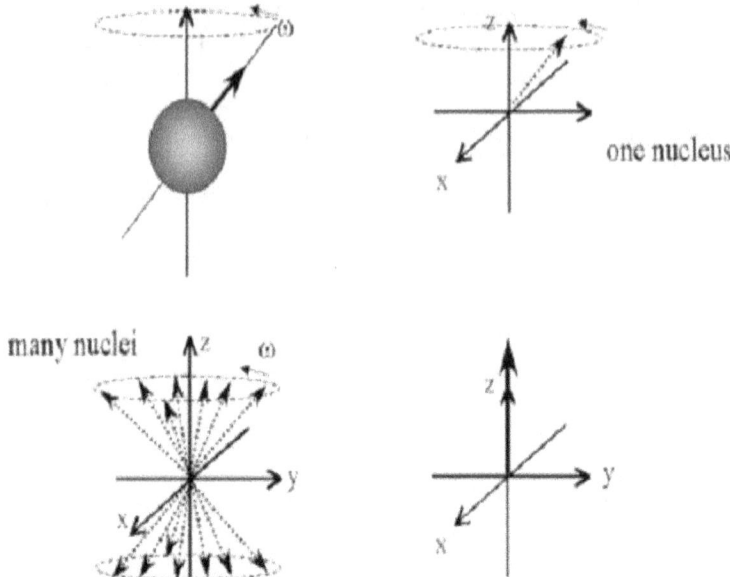

Figure 2: ω indicates the Larmour frequency.

7. Write down possible values m can have for the proton. Draw the scheme.

A proton has spin 1/2, the sum of different values of m is therefore (2 · 1/2 + 1) 2, which gives m = I and -I, ergo +1/2 and -1/2.

$$I = 1/2$$

E $\quad\quad$ $^1H, ^{13}C$

$m = -1/2$ (β) ———— $E_\beta = +1/2\, \gamma\hbar B_0$

0

$m = +1/2$ (α) ———— $E_\alpha = -1/2\, \gamma\hbar B_0$

8. Write down possible values m can have for a nucleus with I=1. Draw the scheme.

+1, 0 and -1.

$I=1$

$^{2}H, ^{14}N$

E

$m=-1$ ———— $E_{-1}= \gamma \hbar B_0$

$m=0$ ———— $E_0=0$

$m=+1$ ———— $E_{+1}=-\gamma \hbar B_0$

$I=1$

$^{2}H, ^{14}N$

$m=-1$ ———— $E_{-1}= \gamma \hbar B_0$

$m=0$ ———— $E_0=0$

$m=+1$ ———— $E_{+1}=-\gamma \hbar B_0$

9. Explain α- and β-spin states of spin-1/2 nuclei. Draw the scheme.

Due to directional quantization only certain angles of the precessing nuclear dipole are allowed. α-spin is with positive magnetic quantum number (m= + 1/2) and β-spin with negative (m = -1/2).

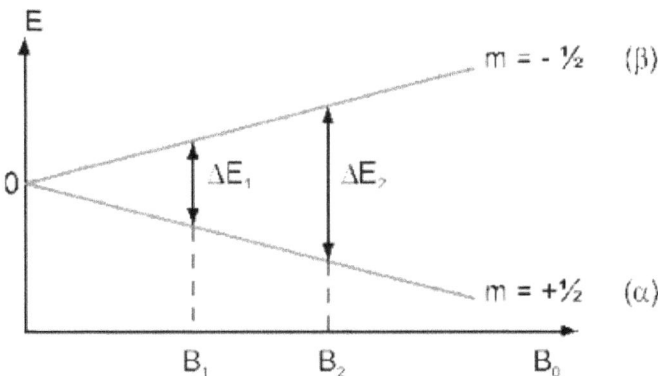

10. Write down the equation for energy difference between two adjacent energy levels of magnetic dipole in an external magnetic field.

$$\Delta E = \gamma \hbar B0$$

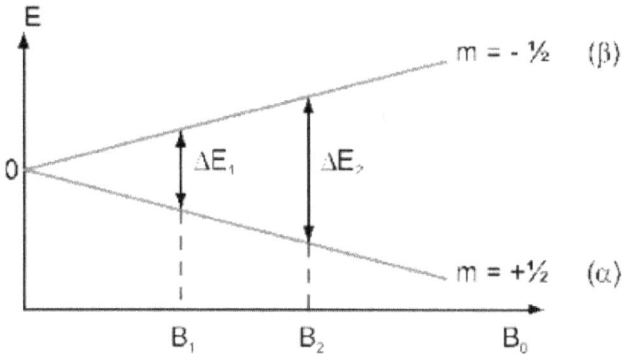

Figure 4: Energy level difference due to **B₀** illustrated.

11. What is the saturation?

Saturation is when the N-populations are equal ($N\alpha=N\beta$). The population is greater in the lower energy level, and this leads to the transition from the lower to the higher level to become the dominant process and is therefore observed signal. The process of moving up in energy requires absorption of energy, while the transition down requires emission. Under saturation the absorption and emission are equal in intensity and cancel each other out, and thus no signal is observed. Used for broadband decoupling, and selective removal of signals.

12. What is the pulse?

The pulse is the radiofrequency pulse that excites all nuclei of one species simultaneously. It contains a band of frequencies symmetrical about the center frequency $\nu1$, with a fixed duration τP (usually several μs).

13. What happens with microscopic magnetizations after the 90∘ pulse?

A small fraction of the microscopic magnetizations (nuclear angular momenta P) are now processing around the z-axis in phase coherence. These results direction. On top of this the number of angular momenta in alpha state is equal to that in the beta state, which results in the disappearance of the macroscopic magnetization in the z direction.

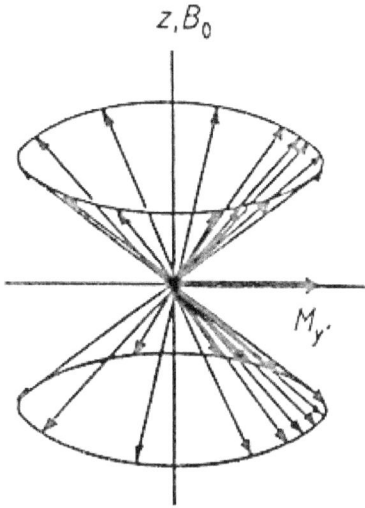

Figur 5: Macroscopic magnetization after a 90 pulse.

14. What is the relaxation?

Immediately after a pulse the spin system will start to revert to its equilibrium state. This is relaxation. Relaxation occurs as transverse (spin-spin) and longitudinal (spin-lattice). The dipoles will dephase, reducing M_y until zero, restoring their random distribution in precession around the z-axis. $N\alpha$ and $N\beta$ return to their equilibrium state, gradually increasing M_z. (See textbook Figure 1-14, page14)

15. What is the purpose of the Fourier transformation?

Its purpose is to transform the time domain spectrum, the FID, recorded during analysis into readable data in the frequency domain.

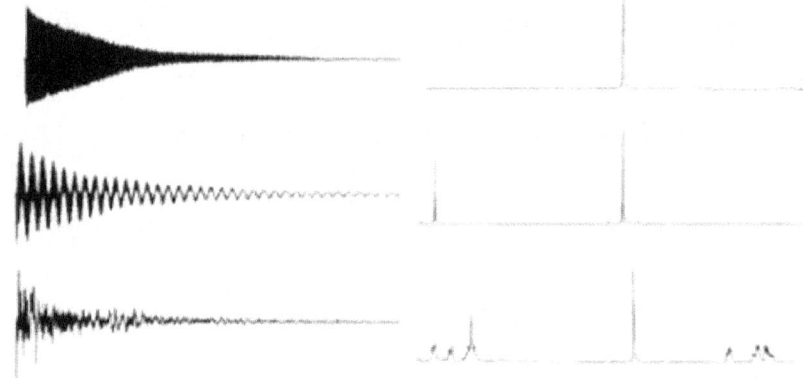

Figur 6: A few FID with their corresponding fourier transformed spectras in the frequency domain.

16.   Write down the expression showing the dependence of the S/N ratio on the number of scan.

The signal/noise-ratio is proportional to the number of scans performed.

S:N = *pNS*

S:N = Signal to noise ratio NS = Number of scans

17. Give a list of main parts of a pulse NMR instrument.

Magnet: Cryomagnets capable of a frequency up to 900 MHz in protons. (21,14Tesla, Hz is relative to the nuclei in question)Probe-head: Where the sample is inserted.

Transmitter: Radiofrequency generator and frequency synthesizer. Also capable of pulse production.

Receiver: Radiofrequency voltage proportional to the transverse magnetization **M***y0* is induced in the receiver coil.

Computer: Digitizes the information and (Fourier) transforms it to readable data.

18. What is the chemical shift?

128

The effect of the magnetic field (B_{eff}) on a specific molecule is always less than the applied field (B_0). This is due to shielding effect (σ) on the nuclei which is analyzed. As nuclei are shielded differently due to their molecular environment they will give separate resonance signals in the spectrum, creating a specific chemical shift for specific nuclei. The different Larmour frequencies of the nuclei result in different chemical shifts.

19. What is the scalar coupling?

It is the interval between the two signals of a doublet. It's the splitting of a signal due to interactions through the chemical bonds. J coupling.

20. What is the zero-order spectrum?

It is a spectrum containing only singlet.

21. What is the first-order spectrum?

It is a spectrum containing multiplets which follow the multiplet rules, meaning that the shape of the multiplets is of consequent size and shape (1:1, 1:2:1, 1:3:3:1 etc. . . Pascals' triangle.) and where the frequency interval between nuclei is large compared to the coupling constant ($\Delta v >> J$).

22. What is the spectrum of higher order?

It is a spectrum containing multiplets which does not follow the multiplet rules. The condition $\Delta v >> J$ is not met, altering the intensity ratios within the multiplets (no longer following Pascals' model) causing additional lines to appear in the spectra and making it more complex.

23. What are integrals?

The area of each signal. In 1H NMR the integrals corresponds with the relative amount of nuclei with the same chemical shift. Integrals from 13C NMR is generally not accurate due to NOE.

24. Why is it necessary to use deuterated solvents for NMR experiments?

Because the proton signal from non-deuterated solvents will easily overshadow any signals from your sample. In addition, it's necessary to have nucleus for the locking of the signal. In polysaccharides the deuturated solvent can exchange the protons of the OH-groups with deuterium, making the spectra a lot easier to interpret.

25. Which tasks an NMR probe has to perform?

Transmitting and receiving signals, decoupling, locking, generating field gradients and amplification of signals.

26. Presence of paramagnetic impurities is mostly unwanted for NMR experiments. Why, what is a typical paramagnetic impurity and how it is usually removed from the sample?

Paramagnetic impurities shorten relaxation time and thereby increase band broadening. Nuclei interacting with impurities may also have its shift moved. Dissolved oxygen is a typical impurity and is removed by degassing the sample.

27. When and why are paramagnetic compounds deliberately added to the sample before running an NMR experiment?

It may be used to remove nuclear overhauser effect but also to change the shifts in order to aid spectral analysis. If the molecule contains many similar, overlapping shifts which are hard to discern, addition of paramagnetic compound may chelate with the molecule and change its shifts so that they are discernable.

28. What is locking and what is its purpose?

Ensures the necessary field frequency stability. If there is no resonance condition, the lock unit applies a field correction until resonance is restored.

29. What is the phase correction?

It removes the dispersion component signals.

30. Which requirements a good NMR solvent has to satisfy?

Good solubility of sample, stable, isotope-labeled (deuterated), non-reactive with sample and have low viscosity. Easily removable solvents may be preferred if the compound is to be retrieved after analysis. Traces of water should be avoided as residual HDO can give broad peaks. 13C-solvents should not overlap with sample.

31. What is the purpose of using shift reagents in NMR?

If the molecule contains many similar, overlapping shifts which are hard to discern, addition of a shift reagent may chelate with the molecule and change its shifts so that they are discernable similar to paramagnetic compound addition.

32. Is it possible to distinguish enantiomers by NMR?

Not without further action. A chiral lanthanide shift reagent or a chiral diamagnetic reagent may be added to form diastereomers. The different diastereomeric complexes may then be distinguished by their different resonances.

33. What is always the result of the rapid dynamic processes on proton NMR spectrum?

They lead to a simplification of the spectrum.

34. The chemical shift scale on a NMR spectrum is typically given in dimensionless units termed "parts per million" (ppm) from some reference compound. What is the relationship between a chemical shift scale in Hz. and a scale in "ppm" ?
Ans

The resonance frequency of a nucleus (expressed in Hz) is directly proportional to the strength of the applied magnetic field and changes from spectrometer to spectrometer, depending on the strength of the magnet. It is more convenient to express the resonance frequency in dimensionless units (termed "parts per million" or "ppm") by dividing the actual resonance frequency of the nucleus by the Larmor frequency of the type of nucleus being observed. In this way, all chemical shifts are effectively "normalised" to take account of the fact that each different spectrometer may have a different magnetic field strength. Chemical shifts are typically measured relative to the frequency of some standard compound, taken by convention as a reference, and chemical shifts are usually expressed in units of ppm from the resonance of the reference compound. Chemical shifts expressed in ppm are independent of Bo and are tabulated as characteristic molecular properties. If the Larmor frequency for observing a nucleus in particular spectrometer is 400 MHz then 1 ppm corresponds to 400Hz.

35. In NMR spectrometers commonly used in medicine, the resonance frequency for the protons in water is 60MHz. If such

an instrument was to be used to observe 31P, what frequency of Rf. radiation would be required?

Ans

The answer to this question requires an understanding of the Larmor equation. One of the things that are obvious from the Larmor equation is that the resonance frequency the higher the magnetogyric ratio, the higher the frequency required observing the NMR signal of the nucleus. The question asks for a comparison between the frequencies required for the observation of protons (1H) and phosphorus (31P) in the same magnet. The magnetogyric ratio of 31P is 0.405 times that of 1H so the frequency required toobserve 31P will be scaled by the same factor:

^{31}P frequency = 1H frequency x 0.405

$\quad\quad$ = (0.405 x 60) MHz = 24.3 MHz

36. In a magnetic field of strength 2.349 T, the resonance frequency of 15N nuclei is 10.13 MHz What is the resonance frequency of 15N in a magnet of 11.745T ?

Ans. The answer to this question again requires an understanding of the Larmor equation. From the Larmor equation, the resonance frequency required to observe a certain type of nucleus is proportional to the strength of the magnetic field (Bo). The higher the magnetic field, the higher the resonance frequency of a given type of nucleus. The question asks for a comparison between the frequencies required for the observation of 15N in two different magnets. The magnetic field strength is increased by a factor of (11.745/2.349) = 5 so the frequency required observing 15N will be scaled by this factor: 15N frequency at 11.745T = 15N frequency at 2.349T x 5 = (10.13 x 5) MHz = 50.65 MHz

37.What would happen to the widths of the 1H NMR signal in a sample of CH₃Br when :

- **A soluble Fe(III) salt was added to the solution.**
- **The solution was scrupulously deoxygenated before the spectrum was acquired.**
- **The solution was cooled to near its freezing point.**

Ans

1. Fe(III) is paramagnetic so a soluble paramagnetic salt in an NMR sample will efficiently relax the nuclei in the sample. Nuclei which relax rapidly give rise to broad signals in the NMR spectrum.

2. Oxygen is paramagnetic and even small amounts of oxygen dissolved in the sample contribute to relaxation. So if the sample was rigorously degassed, this would remove oxygen and the lines would get sharper because the relaxation would be less efficient.

3 .When a solution is cooled to near its freezing point, it becomes viscous and less mobile. Solutes dissolved in the solution are less mobile and tumble more slowly as the viscosity is increased. Relaxation is more efficient when molecular motion is slowed so lines become broader as the solution becomes more viscous.

38. An NMR sample contains protons with both relatively short (say 100 ms) and long (say 10 sec) relaxation times. What would be the qualitative appearance of a series of 1 H NMR spectra of the sample acquired rapidly (say successively at intervals of 4 seconds)?

Ans: If spectra are acquired in quick succession, the signals from the species with the long relaxation time will not have sufficient time to relax between acquisitions. On the other hand, the species with the short relaxation time would be fully relaxed between acquisitions. In the first spectrum, the intensity of signals would exactly represent the concentration of species giving rise to them since the nuclei are fully relaxed prior to acquisition. For the second spectrum (4 seconds later) the nuclei with relaxation time 100 ms will be fully relaxed and will give a signal which is identical to the first spectrum. However the nuclei with long T1 will not be fully relaxed by the time the second spectrum is recorded and the signal intensity will therefore be less. The effect is re-enforced in the 3rd, 4th etc spectrum so after many acquisitions, the intensity of the signals from rapidly relaxing nuclei is relatively accurately defined however the signals from slowly relaxing nuclei will be underestimated.

39.. The 1H NMR spectrum of an organic molecule is usually sharp with resonances which have lines < 0.3 Hz wide. A 2H NMR spectrum of the same sample typically has resonances which are significantly broader with lines approximately 1 Hz (or more) in width. Rationalize this difference.

Ans: The 2H spectrum is broader because the relaxation times of 2H nuclei are always shorter than for 1H. This arises because 2H has a spin of 1. Nuclei with spin other than ½ are called quadrupolar nuclei and relaxation in quadrupolar nuclei is dominated by the presence of the quadrupole. Quadrupolar relaxation, for some quadrupolar nuclei, can be so efficient that the NMR spectra are broadened to the extent that they can't be detected.

40. Why do we see peaks?

When the excited nuclei in the beta orientation start to relax back down to the alpha orientation, a fluctuating magnetic field is created. This fluctuating field generates a current in a receiver coil that is around the sample. The current is electronically converted into a peak. It is the relaxation that actually gives the peak not the excitation.

41. Why do we see peaks at different positions?

Realize that in principle, a peak will be observed for every magnetically distinct nucleus in a molecule. This happens because nuclei that are not in identical structural situations do not experience the external magnetic field to the same extent. The nuclei are shielded or deshielded due to small local fields generated by circulating sigma, pi and lone pair electrons.

42. What causes splitting?

Many peaks in NMR spectra appear as symmetric patterns called doublets, triplets, quartets, quintets, etc. When you see these patterns it tells you about the number of adjacent (usually on the carbon next door to that bearing the absorbing hydrogen(s)), but different hydrogens

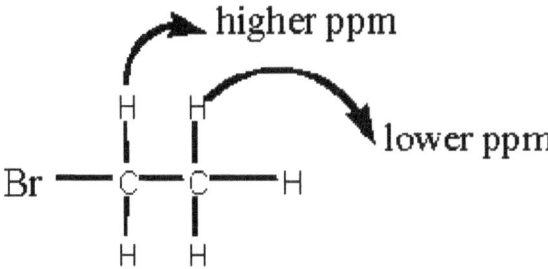

Bromoethane has two different types of hydrogens so we expect two absorptions in the NMR spectrum. One absorption corresponds to the two hydrogens that are closest to the halogen atom. The other to the hydrogens comprising the methyl group that is farther away. Based on its chemical shift, the hydrogens nearer the bromine should be at a higher ppm position. The hydrogens further from the bromine should be at lower ppm position. The hydrogens closer to the bromine will appear as a quartet because they are near three different hydrogens (the hydrogens on the methyl group). Those adjacent hydrogens are communicating their presence to the hydrogens being flipped.

43. What is mean by the term 'Order of NMR Spectrum'?

NMR spectrum reveals three important, fundamental and characteristics features. (i) Chemical shift, (ii) Peak intensity and (iii) Spin couplings. All these parameters are measurable quantities and are considered as the first order of pattern of NMR spectrum. 1H NMR spectra have broadly classified into two main groups on the basis of first order criteria as (i) first order or simple spectra from which the three useful parameters can be deduced and (ii) second order or complex spectra from which the above parameters cannot be easily deduced.

44. What are essential criteria for the first order spectrum?

All essential criteria for first order NMR spectrum are:

(i)　The number of peak into which a band slot is equal to $(n+1)$, where n is the number of adjacent non-equivalent protons causing split.

(ii)　Intensity of signals i.e. relative area under the peaks, are given by the coefficient preceding each term in the expansion formula of $(x+1)^x$ Where n is the number of adjacent non-equivalent protons.

(iii)Chemical shift can be easily deduced from spectrum.

(iv)The ratio of chemical shift difference between the coupling protons express (in Hz) and coupling constant (in Hz) should be equal to or greater than 10 i.e.

$\Delta \delta/J \geq 10$

(v)　Chemically equivalent protons are also magnetically equivalent.

45. How will you distinguish followings by NMR:-
(i) cis and trans-stilbene
(ii) o-dichlorobenzene and p-dichlorobeneze
(iii) Cyclohexanol & chlorocyclohexane
Ans: (i)

cis-stilbene   trans-stilbene

In trans-stilbene, H_b proton is deshielded by both the aromatic ring but in cis-stilbene it is deshielded by only one aromatic ring. So H_b appear at higher field ($\delta \sim 7.0$) and H_a appears at lower field($\delta \sim 6.5$).

(ii) o-dichlorobenzene and p-dichlorobeneze

o-dichlorobenzene   p-dichlorobenzene

0-dichlorobenzene having two types of proton so there is two NMR signal for it whereas in p-dichlorobenzene there is only one types of proton so it shows only single peak.

(iii) **Cyclohexanol & chlorocyclohexane**

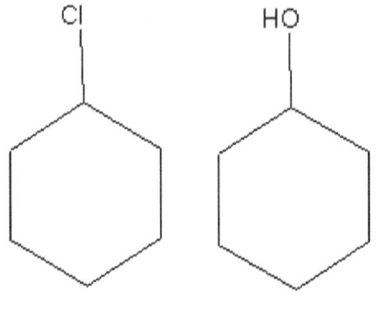

Chlorocyclohexane   Cyclohexanol

Cyclohexanol only undergoes acetylation with $(CF_3CO)_2O$ and then different NMR spectrum is observed.

46. Distinguish of different Isomers of $C_4H_8O_2$ by NMR.

- **Propyl methanoate**
- **ethyl ethanoate**
- **Methyl, propanoate**
- **Butanoic acid**
  Ans: All NMR peaks can be seen in given spectra:

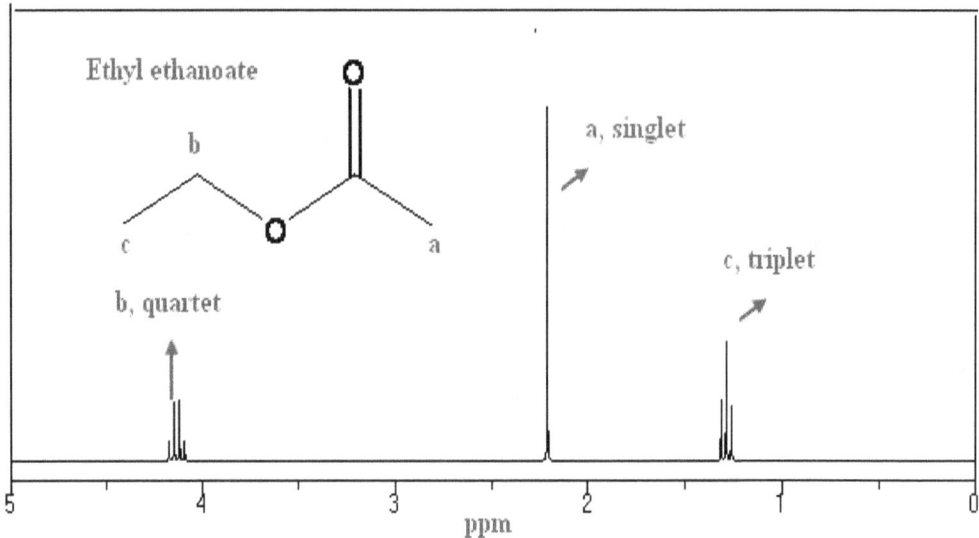

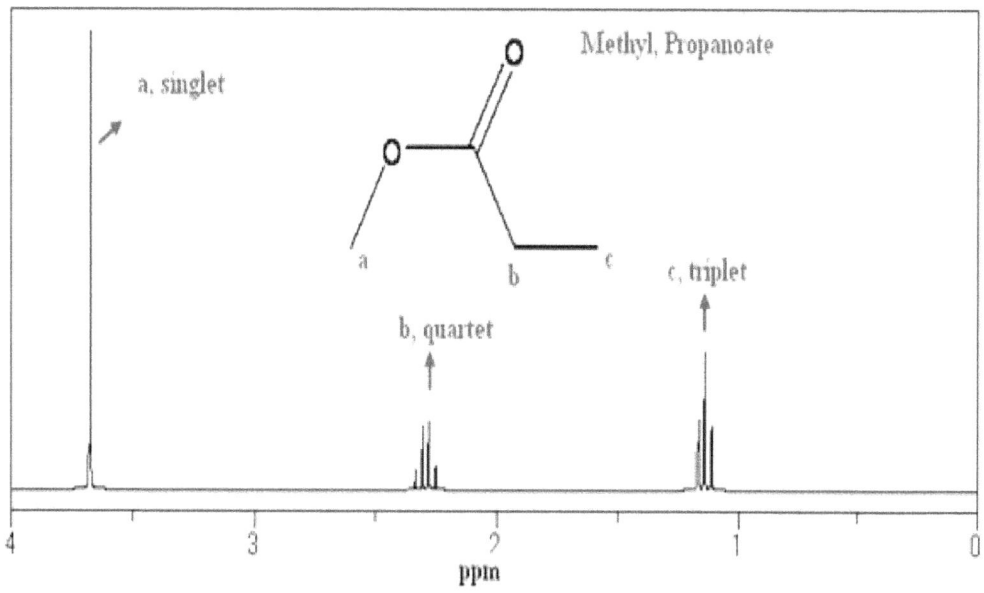

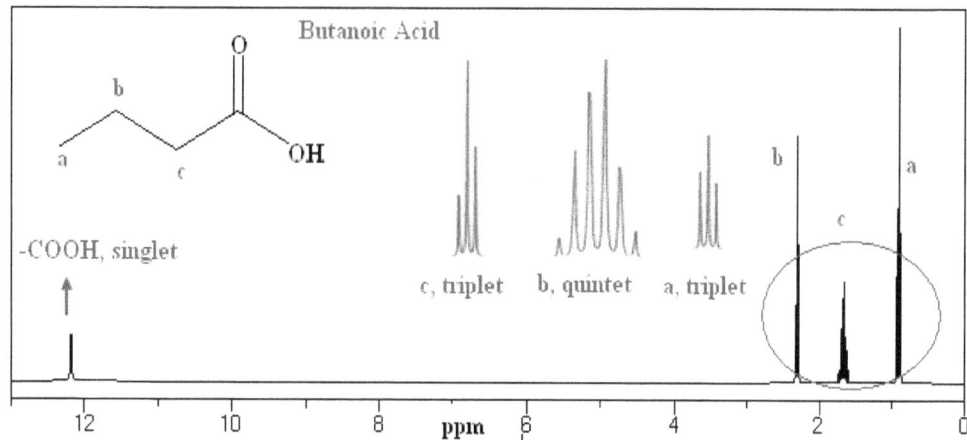

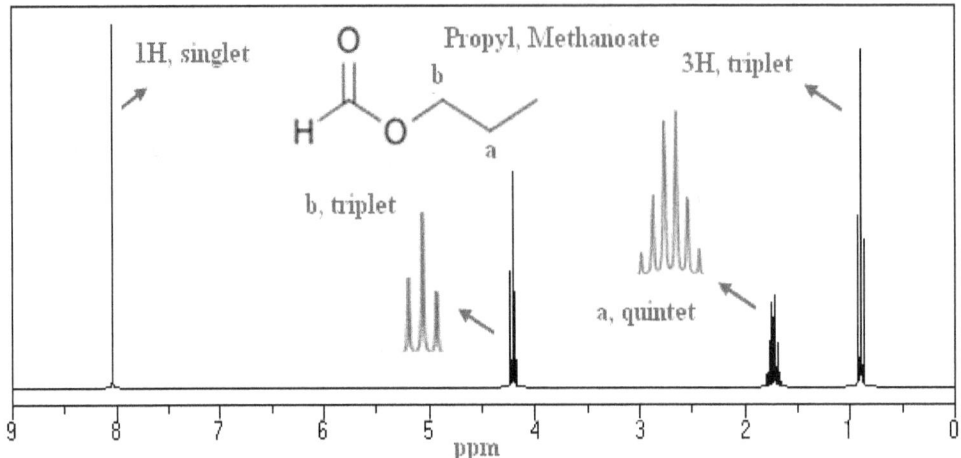

47. Distinguish of different Isomers of $C_5H_{10}O_2$ by NMR
- **Propyl acetate**
- **Methyl butyrate**

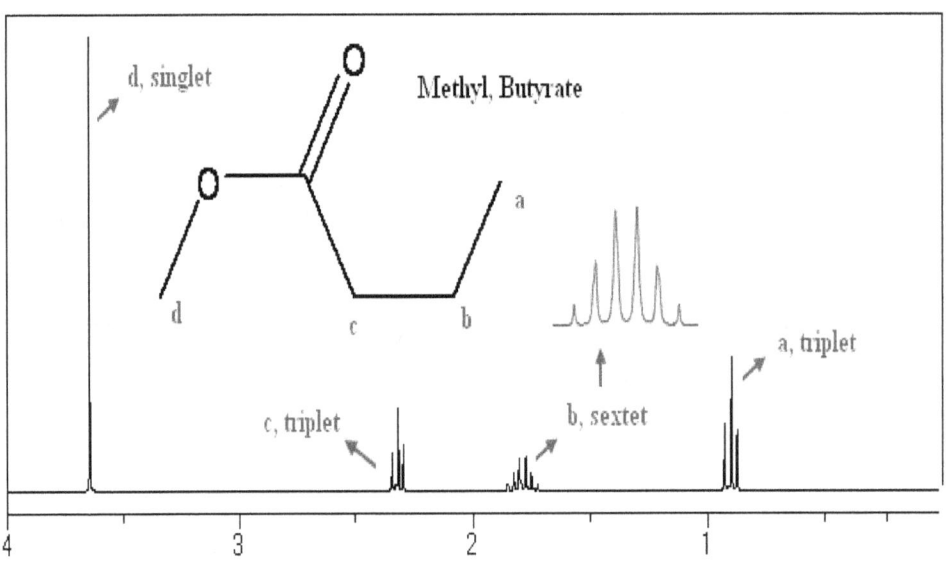

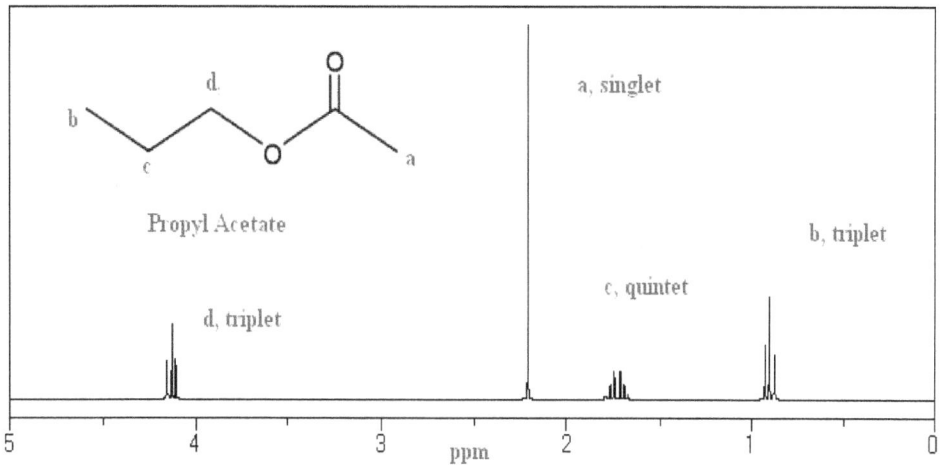

48. How will you distinguish, ethane, ethene and acetylene by NMR.

As ethane, ethene and acetylene contains only one types of proto and so it will show only single NMR signal. Due to different types of environment present there so their peaks position can be identified as:

$$H_3C\!\!-\!\!CH_3 \quad \delta \quad 0.9$$

$$H_2C\!\!=\!\!CH_2 \quad \delta \quad 5$$

$$H\text{-}C\!\equiv\!C\text{-}H \quad \delta \quad 2.5$$

50. Acetylenic protons appear at higher field than ethylenic protons.

An ethylene molecule when placed in a applied magnetic field, the plane of the pi(π) bond lies at right angle to the direction of the applied field. The induced field generated is paramagnetic in the region of the protons and so ethylenic protons appear at lower field.

143

On the other hand acetylinic protons when place in the applied field , becomes oriented in such a manner that the plane of triple bond lies parallel to the direction of the applied field and the induced magnetic field generated due to the circulation of cylindrical electrons of tripled bond opposes the applied field is diamagnetic towards acetylenic protons. Thus acetylienic protons experience smaller field strength and so resonate at higher field.

52. How will you distinguish pri sec and tert alcohol by ^{1}H NMR.

The three types of alcohols can be differentiated by taking ^{1}HNMR spectra in DMSO-d_6 when protons of –OH appears as triplet, doublet and singlet respectively for pri, sec and tert alcohols.

53. What are commonly used solvents for NMR spectroscopy?

The most commonly used NMR solved is $CDCl_3$. IN this solvent most of polar and non-polar compounds are soluble. It is volatile and can be easily removed from sample

Some other solvents are :

- CCl_4: it is used for certain acid –sensitive compounds.
- DMSO-d_6: It is relatively non-volatile and so it may suitable for working at high temperature upto 140°C.
- D_2O: It is highly polar and mainly ued for salts. It can readily change all acidic protons.
- CF_3COOH: It is especially useful for amine and heterocyclic compounds.

54. How does electronegativity affect chemical shift?

The electron cloud shields the nucleus from the applied magnetic field, and electro negativity is defined as the tendency of an atom to pull electrons toward itself. Therefore, electronegative atoms remove electron density from the proton. This causes the proton to have less electron density, and this leads to less shielding. If the proton has less shielding, it will feel the applied magnetic field more, and this leads to a higher energy and a higher chemical shift. Protons that are closer to the electronegative atom are in a less electron dense environment, which means that their chemical shifts will be larger.

55. Explain NMR Spectra of -OH and -NH Protons

The chemical shifts of OH and NH protons vary over a wide range depending on details of sample concentration and substrate structure. The shifts are very strongly affected by hydrogen bonding, with strong downfield shifts of H-bonded groups compared to free OH or NH groups. Thus OH signals tend to move downfield at higher substrate concentration because of increased hydrogen bonding (see the spectra of ethanol below)

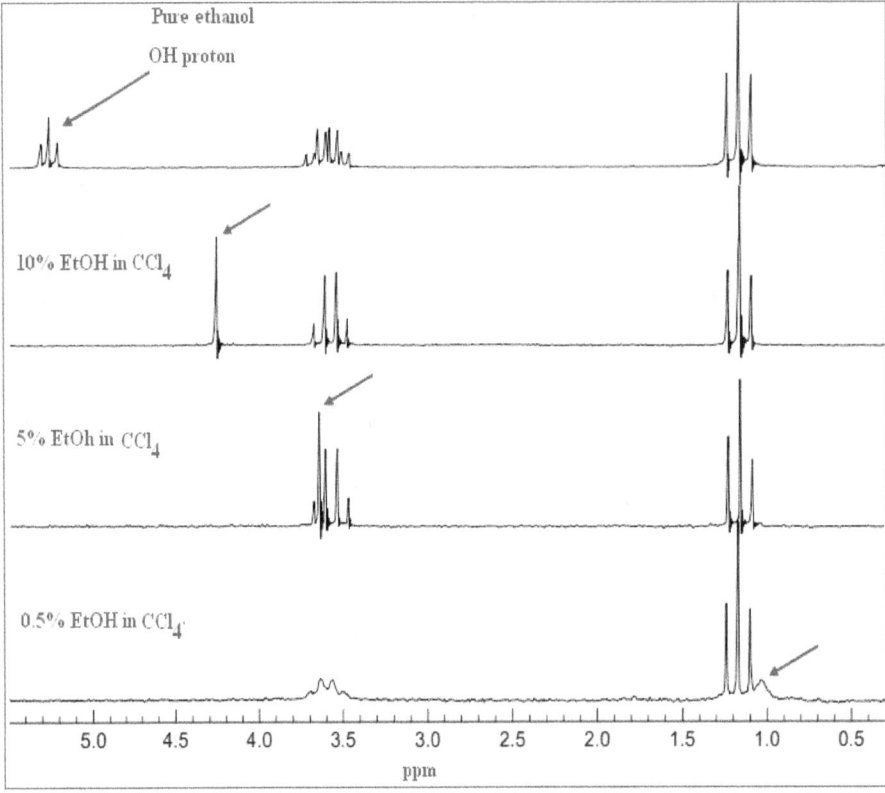

There is a general tendency for the more acidic OH and NH protons to be shifted downfield. This effect is in part a consequence of the stronger H-bonding propensity of acidic protons, and in part an inherent chemical shift effect. Thus carboxylic amides and sulfonamides NH protons are shifted well downfield of related amines, and OH groups of phenols and carboxylic acids are downfield of alcohols.

56. What are characteristic chemical shifts?

An important concept to understand is that similar functional groups have similar chemical shifts. Characteristic chemical shifts are the averages for the normal or typical proton. Therefore, this number varies between different molecules. We cannot use these shift numbers to assign proton types to NMR signals. On the characteristic proton NMR chemical shifts table, two molecules with the same functional group may have different chemical shifts. This could be due to many factors such as being positioned near an electronegative atom.

57. What is magnetic anisotropy and how does it influence chemical shifts?

Magnetic anisotropy is the magnetic field created by pi electrons or rings. This describes an environment where different magnetic fields are found at different points in space. Pi (π) electrons are held less strongly than sigma electrons, so pi electrons are more able to move in response to the magnetic field. How this affects the chemical shift depends on the direction of the induced magnetic field relative to the direction of the applied magnetic field. In pi electrons found in the benzene ring and an alkene, the magnetic field induced is in the same direction as the applied magnetic field, so the protons feel a larger effective magnetic field. Therefore, the protons undergo resonance at a higher frequency due to the pi electrons. If the magnetic field induced is oriented in the opposite direction as the applied magnetic field, the protons will feel a smaller effective magnetic field.

58. Find the number of NMR signals obtained for (a) catechol (b) resorcinol and (c) hydroquinone by giving their NMR spectra.

Ans:

(a) Catechol : 3 signals

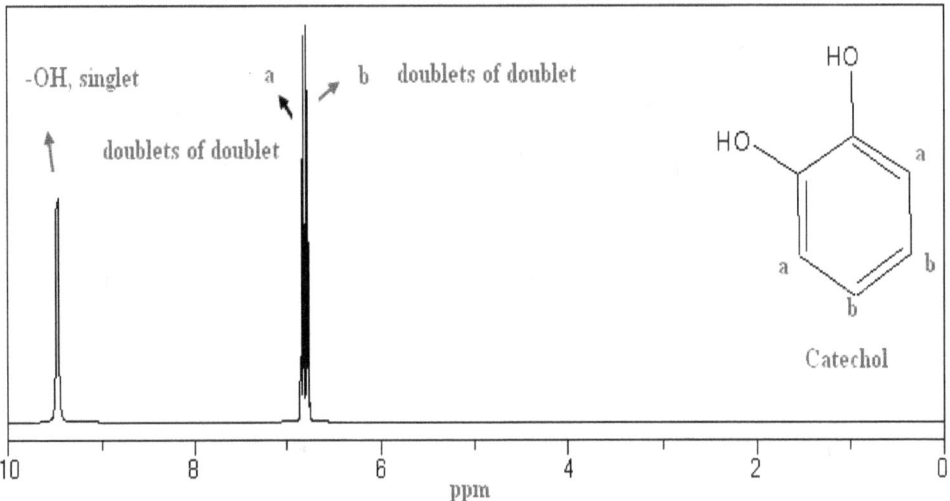

(b) Resorcinol: 4 signals

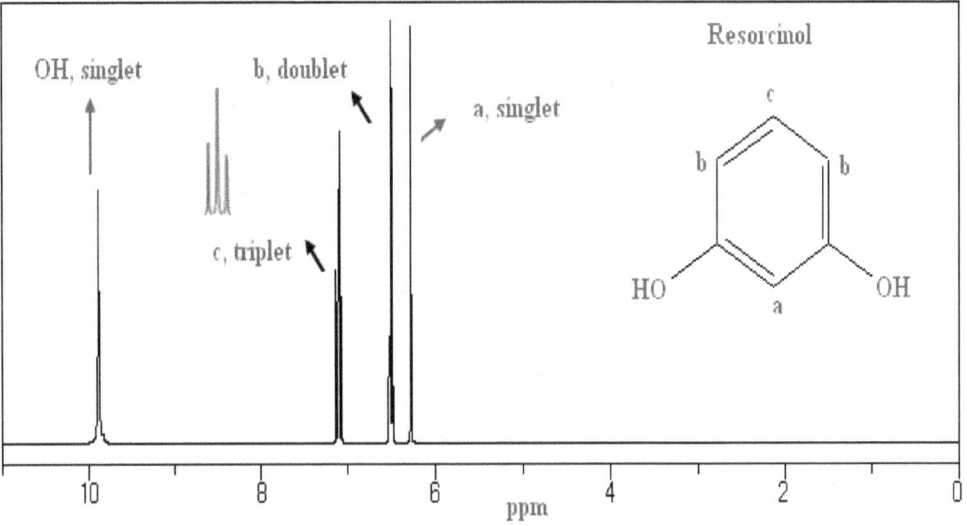

(c) Hydroquinone - 2 signals

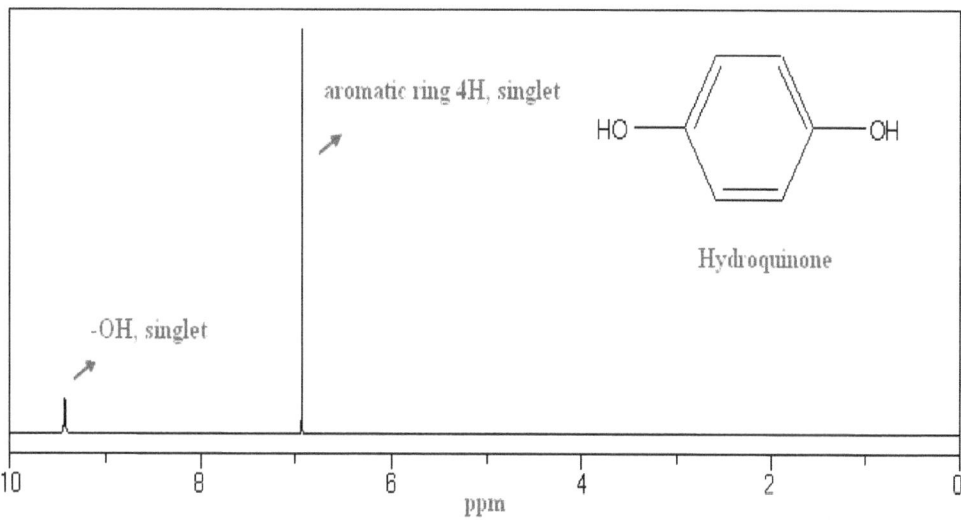

aromatic ring 4H, singlet

-OH, singlet

Hydroquinone

59. Give NMR spectrum of given compound and also assign each peaks:

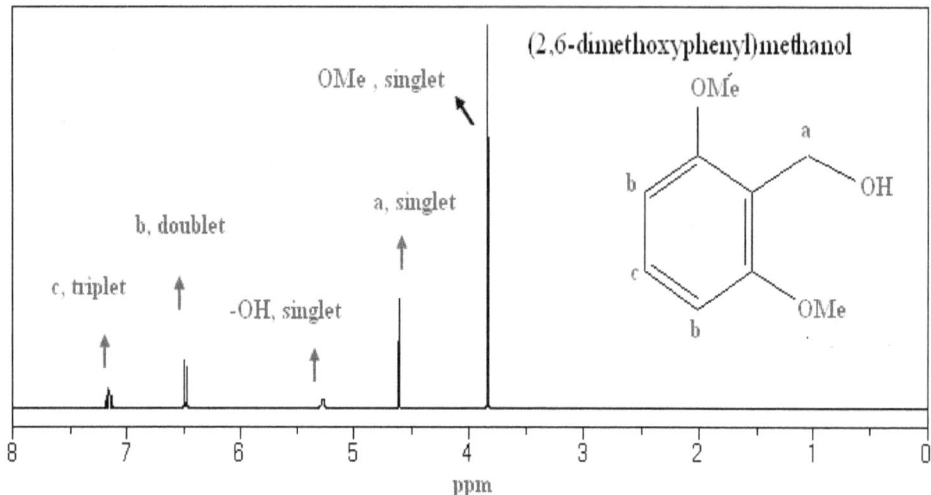

60. How many signals would you expect in the NMR spectrum of phenacetin?

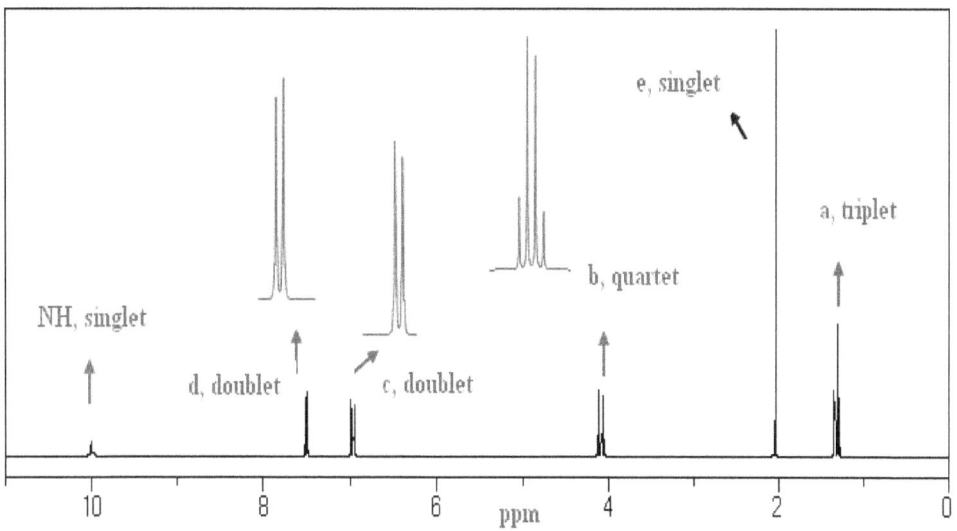

61. How will you distinguish types of hydrogen bonding by ¹HNMR?

Intermolecular H-bonding is concentration and temperature dependent. The extent of hydrogen in the concentration solution will be more and as a results deshielding of protons will more and resonance occurs at higher δ value. On dilution the degree of H-bonding decreased and proton resonate at lower δ value.

While intramolecular H-bonding does not affect the values of chemical shift on dilution.

REFERENCES

1. Organic Spectroscopy through solved problems, D S Mukherjee & B. Mukhopadhyay, New Central Book Agency, Kolkata, India, 2013.

2. Y.R. Sharma Elementary Organic Spectroscopy, 4th Edition, S. Chand & Company. Ltd., New Delhi, India, 2009.

3. P. S. Kalsi, Spectroscopy of Organic Compounds, 10th Edition, New Age International (P) Ltd., New Delhi, India, 2007.

4. V.K. Ahluwalia, Organic Spectroscopy, 1st Edition, Ane Books Pvt. Ltd. New Delhi, India, 2011.

5. H. Kour, Spectroscopy, 11th Edition 2016, Pragati Prakashan, Meerut, India.

6. Atta-ur-Rahman, M. I. Choudhary, Solving Problems with NMR Spectroscopy, Academic Press Inc. USA 1996.

7. Jeremy K. M. Sanders, Modern NMR Spectroscopy: A Guide for Chemists, 2nd Edition, Oxford University Press, 1993

8. L.D.S. Yadav, Organic Spectroscopy, Anamaya Publisher, New Delhi, India, 2005.

9. Atomic and Molecular Spectroscopy, S.K. Dogra & H.S. Randhawa, Dorling Kindersley (India) Pvt. Ltd. 2015.

10. B. K. Sharma, Spectroscopy, 23rd Edition, Krishna Prakashan Media (P) Ltd. 2014.

11. http://chem.ch.huji.ac.il/nmr/whatisnmr/whatisnmr.html

12. https://www.cis.rit.edu/htbooks/nmr/

13. http://www.chemguide.co.uk/analysis/nmr/lowres.html

14. http://www.chem.ucalgary.ca/courses/350/Carey5th/Ch13/ch13-nmr-html

www.ingramcontent.com/pod-product-compliance
Lightning Source LLC
Chambersburg PA
CBHW080413290526
45791CB00008BA/2253